FIRESIDE

FREEDOM FROM BACKACHES

Lawrence W. Friedmann, M.D.
Lawrence Galton

Illustrations by Joseph Stonehill

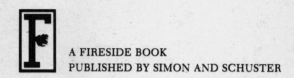

A FIRESIDE BOOK
PUBLISHED BY SIMON AND SCHUSTER

Published by SIMON and SCHUSTER
A Division of Gulf & Western Corporation
Simon & Schuster Building
Rockefeller Center
1230 Avenue of the Americas
New York, New York 10020

Manufactured in the United States of America

1 2 3 4 5 6 7 8 9 10

Library of Congress Cataloging in Publication Data

Friedmann, Lawrence W
    Freedom from backaches.

    (A Fireside book)
    Includes index.
    1. Backache.   I. Galton, Lawrence.   II. Title.
RD768.F7   1979   617'.375   78-26671
ISBN 0-671-21571-X
ISBN 0-671-24853-7 Pbk.

CONTENTS

Is it possible for most backache victims to relieve an acute attack quickly? Determine for themselves the basic cause? And correct it, reducing and even eliminating recurrences?

We think so. More strongly, we know so. And we have tried to make this a complete and perhaps a somewhat unusual book.

You will find in it the answers to such questions as these:

* What is the single most common cause of backaches? What are other common causes? How can you use simple checks and tests to determine whether one of these accounts for your back pain?

* How, when you are in acute pain, can you get prompt relief with simple home measures? Which ones, in what combinations, in what order?

* How, if such measures for relief fail, can you apply new and even unconventional ones, including a modified form of acupuncture and a strange but sometimes useful technique called zone therapy?

* How, once you have made your own diagnosis and achieved relief for yourself, can you prescribe your own home program—specific, tailored to your individual needs, simple, not

excessively time-consuming—to minimize or even eliminate recurrences?

* If you should be one of those in the minority, a relatively small but important minority, who needs medical aid, or one of those in the far smaller minority who needs surgical help, how can you know that you do? Where can you find the kind of help you need?

On any day, 6,500,000 people in this country suffer from bad backs. Much of that suffering is needless. Our purpose in this book is to show what expert medicine, when it is needed, is now capable of accomplishing. It is also to show what many if not most backache victims can successfully do for themselves.

The book is based upon the experience of many specialists at major medical centers concerned with the treatment of back disorders, with investigation of causes and mechanisms, and with finding new and more effective methods of correcting causes.

It is based, too, on the medical author's clinical and research experience as Medical Director of the ICD Rehabilitation and Research Center in New York, the oldest rehabilitation center in the country, which is professionally affiliated with the New York University School of Medicine and collaborates with the Columbia University College of Physicians and Surgeons.

Of the 5,000 patients served yearly at ICD, a sizable proportion come with severe back problems as their sole complaint or as a serious complication of other afflictions. Their need for help has been a constant stimulus to exploring every possible effective method, conventional and unconventional, to relieve chronic back pain, no matter how severe, and to end its chronicity. Happily, success is frequent—and, even more gratifying, the success of late has come increasingly from the efforts of the patients themselves, who quickly learn how to provide their own relief, pinpoint their basic problem, and use simple measures to correct it.

We extend our great appreciation to the many physicians and therapists at ICD who helped develop the techniques we write about here and to the patients who proved they are practical for individual home use.

CHAPTER 1

ALMOST ANY BACKACHE

CAN BE STOPPED

—USUALLY SIMPLY

The late comedian Joe E. Lewis liked to tell a tale of getting a bad back after coming home a bit under the weather. "I saw a spider on the ceiling and tried to step on it," he used to say, and would then go on to relate how he consulted a physician who told him to use hot towels but on the way home stopped for dinner and Arturo, the headwaiter, told him to use cold towels instead.

"Naturally, I used cold towels—and the next time I saw my doctor and told him what happened," Lewis would relate, "he shook his head and said, 'That's funny, the headwaiter at the country club told me to use hot towels.'"

If any backache victim hasn't heard that particular story, he undoubtedly has an equivalent of his own. Of backache jokes, there are plenty, probably more than for any other human affliction. And among all afflictions, backache possesses perhaps the most unusual array of odd qualities.

It almost goes without saying that it is common—almost as common as the common cold. Each year in industry alone, some 400,000 workers suffer disabling back injuries.

But it's hardly necessary to do manual work for a living to acquire a pain in the back. The scenario may vary almost endlessly. Maybe you're wrestling with a spinnaker, or finishing one of those picture-book swings on the second tee, or maybe you're simply opening a window or leaning over to tie a shoelace: no matter, it hits and it's "sproing!" as some victims put it.

Painful? Sharply, intensely, even agonizingly painful. It hurts in the small of the back every time you move—if you can move. Some victims have been known to shuffle, crabwise, to the nearest doctor or emergency room; some have had to be carted from the scene in an ambulance.

To hear many tell it, it doesn't matter whether you then have your back stretched and straightened, or sprayed and heated, or massaged or just looked at. From then on, you're "it." The pain may duly depart in time—but months or even just weeks later, you are bending over the bathroom sink to cold-water yourself into wakefulness, and—sproing!—again it hits. You are now an official chronic bad-backer, one of a legion of millions of Americans, a legion that musters new members at the rate of one and a half to two million annually.

Backache is even fashionable, an "in" misery. "It has emerged as such a status symbol," one popular magazine article a few years ago observed, "that sufferers boldly and openly proclaim their affliction by the way they stand—with pelvis thrust forward and one hand held casually astern in the vicinity of the fifth lumbar region. In suburban do-it-yourself America, where wives stoop to garden or empty the dryer and husbands rake leaves, shovel snow and occasionally build a stone wall, a community's mode of living can be gauged quite precisely by the number of fortyish adults with aches in the back in all their stylish refinements."

It's almost as if backache had become "in" because of a prevailing notion that once a sufferer, always a sufferer, and if one must live with an affliction, one might as well be proud of it.

An old cliché has it that backaches became inevitable once man, millennia ago, learned to stand up on two legs instead of crawl around on all fours. Obviously, however, since millions go through life without ever having a twinge, the inevitability doctrine has to be regarded with some suspicion.

There is also an idea that whatever other progress modern medicine may have made, it has made none at all when it comes to backache. The prevailing notions seem to be that no specific, effective treatments exist for backaches, there are no practical known ways to avoid backaches, most backaches are the results of ruptured disks, and that means surgery, and that is hopeless.

But all of this is nonsense.

THE CASE FOR HOPE: GOOD AND GROWING

The fact is that in the overwhelming majority of instances, backaches have nothing to do with ruptured disks or any other serious organic problems. That statement, unequivocal and meant to be, is based not only on experience with more than 5,000 backache patients treated at the ICD Rehabilitation and Research Center, but also on the experience of physicians who treat backaches regularly as a significant part of their practice, and also on the results of a two-university study of 5,000 backache patients, of which we will have more to say later.

The fact is, too, that major advances have been made in providing relief for virtually all types of backaches, in diagnosing backache causes, in getting at and eliminating the causes, and in preventing endless recurrences.

It is, to be sure, a fact that not all physicians necessarily have an interest in, up-to-date knowledge about, and an ability to help backache patients properly. And we'll have more to say about physicians who do have such interest, knowledge, and ability, and how to find them.

But, beyond that, it is also a fact that backache victims themselves often can—and a major purpose of this book is to help them—diagnose the cause or causes of their backaches. They often can give themselves prompt relief, which is the urgent first need. And they very often can correct the cause and prevent recurrences. Nor does this require any special genius.

THE DISK MYTH—AND A FEW OTHERS

Several years ago, a 39-year-old man was referred to ICD after a long history of suffering with severe low back pain. Two years before the referral, he had had a laminectomy and fusion operation for a herniated intervertebral disk, but that had left him with as much pain as before.

By now, the patient was emotionally as well as physically and financially drained. He was a sensitive artist by talent and desire, a taxicab driver because of the need to support his family. But his driving for years had had to be sporadic because of his bad back which, he felt, also was destroying his family life, leaving him unable to have marital relations or even to play with his child.

It was possible to determine, after thorough examination, that the spinal operation had been successful enough in terms of the intervertebral disk—but that it had been in vain because the disk was not his problem.

There is a recently described "pseudodisk" syndrome with all the symptoms and signs of disk herniation when, in fact, there is no herniation. There are also disks that herniate and cause no symptoms whatever. The dictum of "post hoc ergo propter hoc" is often fallacious. Because a person has a herniated or degenerated intervertebral disk and then experiences back pain doesn't necessarily mean that the back pain comes from the disk.

This patient's pain stemmed from a totally different cause—a notably weak abdominal muscular system with protuberant abdomen and excessive lordosis or swayback—nicely calculated, given a bit of encouragement by some sudden, unusual motion or strain, to produce exquisite backache and, unless corrected, to make the backache a chronic problem.

The first need was to get rid of the immediate acute pain—which could be achieved, as it almost invariably can be, with proper professional help, but it often can be done by patients themselves with measures to be discussed later.

What was needed after the immediate pain was abolished was a planned corrective program, but it was difficult for the patient to get started on it. Understandably, after years of pain and a useless operation, he was terrified of moving, since movement had so often led to agony. It took several months just to convince him that he could move with relatively little pain and could carry out corrective exercises. After eight months, he was back at work full time—really double full time, with one shift of cab driving and another of painting, which was what he wanted.

Another interesting case, an earlier one that taught the medical author something he will never forget, came when he was just beginning to learn the specialty of physical medicine and was studying under Dr. Allan Russek of New York University.

One day, Dr. Russek placed a set of x-rays on a view box and asked, "Larry, what do you think about this man's problem? What do you think he should be capable of doing?"

I looked at the x-rays of the spine and was horrified. The bones of the spine resembled a set of irregular stones, with no

apparent relationship to a normal spine. Almost all the intervertebral disks had degenerated; loose bone fragments could be
observed; and there obviously was severe arthritis.

I said, "Allan, I think it would be a miracle if this man could
get in here on anything but a stretcher. I can't see how he can
possibly walk."

Russek smiled, asked the nurse to bring in the next patient,
and in walked a short, stocky man—and he walked with a
vigorous bounce. The man whose x-rays I had just seen?
Russek assured me that he was. He turned out to be a cele-
brated Hungarian fencing instructor who not only continues to
teach fencing but in the summer, because he thoroughly enjoys
it, spends his time in a camp for young boys, teaching them
horseback riding and other vigorous sports as well as fencing.

Is he immune to backache? No. He gets attacks fairly frequently, gets relief quickly with measures we will be dealing
with later, and manages to avoid severe pain and disability
because of his excellent muscular condition.

No backache is ever hopeless, as these cases help to illustrate.
Moreover, more often than not, a backache is unrelated to
herniated disk, arthritis, or other serious organic conditions.

A study carried out by a combined medical group from New
York University and Columbia University covered 5,000 con-
secutive patients with back pain. In 81 percent of the cases, the
back pain was found to have nothing whatever to do with
herniated intervertebral disks, tumors of any kind, or, indeed,
organic conditions of any kind. This large proportion of patients, some 4,000 of the 5,000, had backaches related, simply
if agonizingly, to muscular insufficiency or inadequate flexibility
of muscles and tendons.

It should be stressed that the study included every back-pain
patient seen at the two universities until a total of 5,000 cases
was reached. It was an unselected sample, which means that

the results of the study should apply to the general population, rather than some small group.

And that means that more than three fourths of patients with back pain can be assured that they have no organic disorder causing their pain, that the pain can be relieved without resort to surgery, and that recurrences can be reduced in frequency or severity or both, and may even be eliminated, by relatively simple measures.

Even when a disk problem is involved, there is no inevitable need for surgery. There is a widespread belief that if a disk herniates or degenerates, there is pressure on nerves, and if the pressure and the pain are to be overcome surgery must be done. But many herniated and degenerated disks do not press on nerves. Even those that do are more likely to cause pain in the leg rather than in the back.

Something else is very much worth knowing about disks, nerves, and backaches. When a nerve is compressed, there may be pain. But when the nerve is compressed for an extended period, it stops causing pain because it dies. If pain then continues, it is because of muscle spasm, and the spasm almost invariably can be relieved by nonsurgical means. We shall have much more to say in this book about muscle spasm—about what it is like, its mechanism of action, how it produces pain, how often you can detect the spasm and pinpoint its location for yourself and, often too, overcome it.

But to return, for a moment, to a nerve being pressed upon because of a herniated disk. In some cases, the pressure can be relieved by *heavy* pelvic traction. Ordinary traction in bed, whether at home or in a hospital, is inadequate for this purpose. Maximum traction possible in bed without pulling the patient off the edge of the bed is usually about 15 pounds. Beyond that, friction between the patient's body and the sheets is not enough to hold the patient. But far more traction can be exerted if there is countertraction on the chest wall. For this, special equipment now has been developed. Such devices provide, intermittently, traction and countertraction up to 200 pounds. And it is this high level of traction that may be useful in adequately separating the vertebrae so that pressure on nerve roots is relieved. The relief may be obtained with a few treatments; in some cases, a single treatment is enough.

Once the traction treatment is finished and the patient stands and walks, his body weight will tend to press the vertebrae together again. Yet, adequate traction can be effective for this reason: When a nerve is pressed upon, it swells. The bony canal through which it passes doesn't budge, of course. The swollen nerve fills the canal. It can be thought of as compressing itself in the unyielding canal, because of its swollen state. And the swelling is aggravated as pressure on veins and lymphatics blocks the outflow of fluids.

When there is a period, sometimes as brief as 15 minutes, during which traction is adequate to relieve pressure, fluids can flow out and the nerve swelling is reduced. After this, even though the vertebrae move back to close to the same position as before, the reduction of nerve swelling has ended the nerve self-compression, and the total pressure now is markedly less.

NEW—AND UNCONVENTIONAL—MEASURES

The backache problem has two basic aspects. One is how to prevent back pain from ever occurring at all or, if it has occurred, how to minimize the frequency and severity of recurrences and, if possible, stop the recurrences completely. The other is how to relieve acute back pain when it is present, how to get rid of it most quickly and effectively.

It is now clear that in the vast majority of cases the prime cause of backache is muscular inadequacy. Moreover, many studies have underscored the importance to the back not just of muscles in the back but of muscles of the abdomen. Investigators repeatedly have demonstrated that the support provided for the spine by a rigid abdominal cavity and a firm structure of stomach muscles is what makes it possible for people to lift weights that otherwise could break the spine. They have also shown that in ordinary movements, strong abdominal muscles keep the stomach from sagging forward, and it is sagging forward that imposes dangerous stress on the lower, or lumbar, region of the spine.

Actually, the growing awareness of the importance of abdominal muscles has led to change in the type of supportive garments that some backache victims wear. Once they were designed chiefly to prop up the spine; now they are designed to give support to the stomach, to serve as a quasi-replacement for strong abdominal muscles.

And, of course, exercises to strengthen stomach muscles have become a key part of bad-back therapy—theoretically. In reality, exercise programs have palled—and usually quickly—on many who have tried them. To some extent, this could be due to a failure to understand their purpose. Without clear insights into exactly how such programs can help, and without an understanding of other benefits to be expected in addition to a healthier back, it can be difficult to feel motivated to take out a sizable chunk of time each day to spend on exercising.

But, to no small extent, exercise programs have palled because they have required too much time—more time than most people have to give to them.

We shall, later in this book, provide a new program of exercise to prevent back pain—new in the sense only that this is its first detailing in print for the public. Actually, it has been developed and used over a period of many years at ICD. It is effective; it is all the more so because it can be carried out in, at most, two 15-minute periods a day, much less time than other programs have required. Most patients find it easy to stick with and rewarding.

We shall not dismiss briefly the other causes of backache.

They affect fewer than one out of four backache sufferers, but that is still a very large number. And there have been major advances both in recognizing the causes in individual cases and in overcoming them.

Nor shall we be content in this book to dwell only on long-established relief measures for acute back pain. Such measures can be effective in many cases when properly applied and we will be concerned with showing how they work; when, how, and in what order they are best used; and how they may be used effectively at home.

ACUPUNCTURE

But there are also unusual measures for relieving back pain. Some are new to physicians in America, although they have been used for thousands of years elsewhere. One case in point is acupuncture.

Can acupuncture really ease back pain? The Chinese have used it for millennia for that purpose among many other purposes. Until very recently, acupuncture for any purpose was summarily dismissed by Western medicine. Western physicians have demanded a rational theory to explain how acupuncture works—if it works. Oriental physicians agree that there is no such rational theory. Acupuncture works, the Orientals say; how is not clear. And, indeed, lack of a theory to explain its mechanism does not necessarily mean that a treatment is ineffective.

To this day, we have little real knowledge of how aspirin works; it works. Nor, after its use for more than a century, are we entirely certain of how digitalis works for patients with heart failure. Insulin is used to treat diabetes, yet many diabetics produce even more insulin than do normal individuals and still may respond to administered insulin; we have much yet to learn about diabetes and about insulin. Penicillin was used for many years before anyone knew its mode of action, which is bursting the cell walls of bacteria; and, in fact, it is still not entirely clear how penicillin makes the cell walls burst. Nevertheless it kills many disease bacteria.

We became interested at ICD some years ago in acupuncture. There was reason for the interest. We have mentioned before briefly the problem of muscle spasm in backache and we will go into it at greater length later. Associated with muscle spasm is another problem: trigger points. Trigger points seem to be localized areas of muscle edema or swelling which persist for long periods and can produce pain. They have been treated with freezing sprays of ethyl chloride, often with good results. Often, too, injection of medication into trigger points has provided relief. But at ICD we have also found that just needling the trigger points—without injecting anything at all—often provides relief.

And when we investigated acupuncture diagrams, we noted an interesting relationship between acupuncture points and the most frequent sites of trigger points. Since then, we have been progressively studying all traditional acupuncture points in order to determine which might be useful for treating back pain.

In addition, we have explored the possible value of massage over acupuncture points—simple massage with the fingers, with the knuckles, and with hard objects such as hard-rubber instruments and the metallic covers in which some cigars are packaged. We have found that some patients respond well to such treatment—and we have also found that some of these acupuncture points can be massaged at home.

ZONE THERAPY

Another unconventional measure for relieving back pain which we have been investigating is called "zone therapy." Although it was proposed many years ago, it has had little use in this country, and many physicians have never even heard of it.

Zone therapy is based on an idea that pressure on certain parts of the body can relieve discomfort from disease conditions far removed from where the pressure is applied. For example, pressure over points on the fingers, hands or feet can, zone therapy proponents long ago suggested, relieve internal disease discomfort and pain at distant sites such as the head. In this regard, zone therapy is similar to acupuncture, in which needling of certain areas may relieve pain at distant sites.

There is no accepted theory to explain how zone therapy might work. Yet it does on occasion. In a recent case in point, the patient complained of severe pain in the left side of the neck from an old injury. There was extreme muscle spasm, and an ethyl chloride spray relieved it. The patient then complained of pain in the right side of the neck which she had not felt previously. This is not unusual; when multiple areas are painful, a patient commonly pays attention only to the most painful area. But, after the right side of her neck was sprayed, the patient complained of excruciating headache; now, suddenly, her head felt, she said, as if it were really going to explode.

Unable to find any clear reason for the head pain, the medical author took the second and third fingers of her right hand, squeezed hard over the nails and balls of the fingers, without telling her why. When her fingers were released, she was startled to find that the pain in her head had disappeared.

While we cannot explain why, there is no doubt that the finger squeezing relieved the head pain. It may be that the explanation lies in suggestibility on the part of the patient, although a special effort was made to avoid suggesting that the squeezing would do anything for the head pain. And certainly no average person would expect pressure on two fingers to relieve a headache.

There have been similar successes in relieving back pain with zone therapy. It is even possible for some patients to use it at home. In some cases, effects can be achieved simply by wrapping a rubber band around the fingers. Zone therapy will be discussed much more fully in Chapter 7.

Does it make sense to use measures that cannot be explained scientifically? The fact is that although medicine has made great progress on a scientific basis, it is still not, and cannot be, entirely scientific. Much remains to be explored and understood. Medicine must be art as well as science.

The open mind, it seems to us, is vital for both physician and patient. There should be willingness to try any measure that meets at least two criteria: first, that it cause no damage either in itself or by virtue of standing in the way of seeking established, effective treatment; and, second, that it not be unduly costly in terms of money or discomfort, or both.

Not all headaches are relieved by aspirin, nor all disease germs overcome by penicillin. No treatment of any kind is effective for all. And certainly there is no single treatment effective for all cases of backache—yet, almost invariably, some way can be found to relieve back pain. And relief is important both in itself and because it can allow other steps to be taken to get at the cause and eliminate it—especially when, as is so often the case, the cause is not organic and may be simply remedied provided the patient, freed of pain, can start to work at it.

TREATING YOURSELF

At the very least, in three of every four cases, as we have noted, back pain is not linked to any underlying disease; and very often, in such cases, a reasonably intelligent individual can arrive at the correct diagnosis of his problem by using the techniques to be discussed later. There is considerable likelihood, too, that once having arrived at the diagnosis, an intelligent individual can treat the problem—entirely or almost entirely—on his or her own, with measures to be discussed.

It has been said that not only a patient but even a physician who treats himself "has a fool for a patient." Yet this is only partly true. All of us treat ourselves for simple colds and other minor illnesses—and, indeed, if we didn't, physicians would be swamped and unable to handle more serious illnesses.

What must be remembered is that in treating yourself, if the pain does not yield or if it should become more severe, it could be that you have not arrived at a proper diagnosis or you may be doing something wrong in treatment. In that case, expert help is necessary to make certain of the diagnosis and, if that is correct, to determine which particular facets of the treatment you have been using are not appropriate.

CHAPTER 2

WHERE IT HURTS, WHY,

AND WHY IT CAN

HURT SO MUCH

If anyone were looking for a problem with an almost infinite variety of *possible* causes and contributing factors, he would be hard put to find a more suitable candidate than backache.

Note the use of *possible*, not *probable*. For backache, the possibles are many; the probables, accounting for the bulk of all backaches, are few.

This is not a textbook and there will be no overly lengthy dwelling on anatomy. But for an understanding of back pains— what can cause them and what can be done to relieve and prevent them—it's helpful to consider the makeup of the spinal column and associated structures in the back.

THE FUNNY BONE

It's been said that the human back needs special consideration because Nature failed to give it enough.

Just look at it: The spinal column, or backbone, is a column of separate bones or vertebrae. They are not set, one atop another, like a column of toy blocks. Instead, to balance weight, they are arranged in an S-curve. And each vertebra rests on the one below at an angle, depending upon muscles and ligaments to hold it there.

What could be considered even worse from a structural standpoint, the lowest of the lumbar vertebrae perches on the sacrum, which is attached to the pelvis at such an acute angle that only ligaments and muscles prevent the whole spine from slipping forward completely off the pelvis. It may seem like a miracle that we can stand up, an even greater one that we can lift and carry any weights at all.

Now take a closer look:

Stacked upward from the sacrum at the base of the spine to

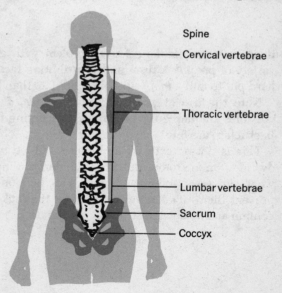

Spine

Cervical vertebrae

Thoracic vertebrae

Lumbar vertebrae

Sacrum

Coccyx

the skull are 33 vertebrae. At the bottom, forming the very end of the spine, is the coccyx, which is really 4 fused coccygeal vertebrae. Next up the ladder come the 5 sacral vertebrae, the portion of the spinal column that joins with the pelvis; the sacral vertebrae also are fused.

The 5 lumbar vertebrae—individual, as are all the rest—come next; they are low in the back. Atop them are stacked the 12 dorsal, or thoracic, vertebrae, which fall in the area behind the chest; and, finally, at the top, are the 7 cervical, or neck, vertebrae.

Although each vertebra is a little different from the others— as the bones stack toward the skull, they decrease progressively in size—all have features in common. Essentially, a vertebra consists of a ring of bone and a solid cylinder of bone. The ring presses into the cylinder, and the rings of all vertebrae together form a tube, the spinal canal, which houses and protects the spinal cord. The cord emerges from the brain and contains nerve cables. Smaller nerve bundles branch off from the cord and run to all parts of the body—muscles, skin, other tissue. They transmit sensations to the brain and from the brain carry orders, including those for the movement of muscles.

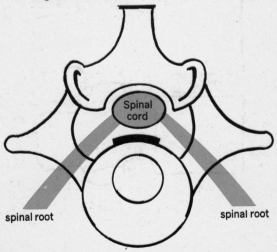

There are differences in the amount of motion possible in different regions of the spine. In both the cervical (neck) and lumbar (low back) regions, movement is relatively free. But the thoracic vertebrae are joined to the ribs, and the ribs in turn are connected to the sternum, or breastbone, which is relatively rigid. The thoracic vertebrae, therefore, have only a small range of motion. Motion is also limited for the sacrum, a fused mass of five vertebrae joined to the pelvis on either side by the sacro-iliac joints, forming the back wall of the pelvic region.

Between each vertebra and the next is a spinal disk, a circular cushion of connective tissue and cartilage, roughly one quarter to three quarters of an inch thick. Each disk consists of several layers of tough, fibrous rings and has, in its center, a softer nucleus.

The spinal disks perform an important function. They serve to absorb the impact of body weight and movements. Normally, they maintain their efficiency as shock absorbers throughout a lifetime.

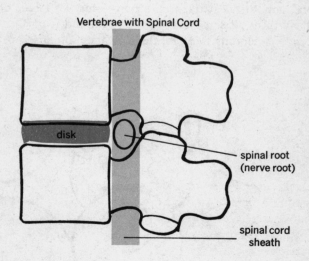

Vertebrae with Spinal Cord

disk

spinal root
(nerve root)

spinal cord
sheath

The vertebrae have no stability of their own. Tough, fibrous ligaments run between and bind them together, much as ligaments connect adjacent bones all over the body. But while the ligaments of the spinal column act as checks, helping to stabilize and to prevent excessive motion, they do not suffice to keep the column upright. It takes muscle action to do that. One indication of the importance of muscles is the immediate collapse because of the interruption in muscle activity when fainting occurs or consciousness is otherwise lost.

In four-legged animals, the spinal column functions much as a suspension bridge, supported by the four legs that serve as four pillars. In man, with two of the pillars, the arms, up in the

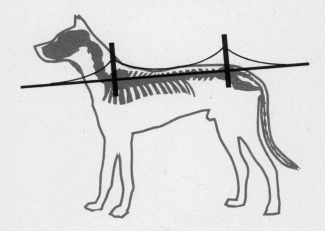

air, balance and stabilization must come, for the most part, from the muscles fore and aft. The stomach muscles as well as the back muscles act much as the guy wires often used to hold young trees erect. The hip muscles also participate in the "guying" of the spine.

There are some 140 muscles attached to the spine and they perform a prodigious amount of work. When, for example, you bend forward so your trunk is flexed 60 degrees from the vertical, the muscle force required to keep you from toppling over, if you weigh, say, 180 pounds, will be 450 pounds. If, in addition, you are carrying a 50-pound weight in this position, the muscles will have to exert a force of 750 pounds. It should be added, too, that under these circumstances, there will be a compression force of some 850 pounds exerted against the fifth lumbar vertebra—and while stress on the spine and its adjacent structures is considerable even during proper lifting, the attempt to lift a 50-pound weight with bent back rather than with bent knees and hips can be truly dangerous.

Beyond supporting the spine, giving it balance, and allowing it to move, the muscles attached to the spine also serve, through their healthy bulk, to provide protection for it.

THE "SLIPPED" DISK

The "slipped" disk problem you so often hear about involves a slip only in terminology, for a spinal disk does not slip. What happens in the case of the so-called slipped disk is that the rim

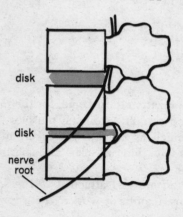

of the disk, the annular ligament, weakens and tears, and part of the soft gelatinlike center, the nucleus pulposus, becomes extruded. The extruded (herniated) portion presses on sensitive nerve roots and produces pain, sometimes so great as to be disabling.

The spinal column, we have noted, houses and protects the fragile spinal cord. Through the cord run bundles of nerves that function, in a sense, as the body's private internal telephone system, relaying messages back and forth between brain and muscles and organs throughout the body, allowing perception of heat, cold, and other sensations, and making possible appropriate reactions to them.

The spinal cord begins where the brain ends at the base of the skull and continues for about 18 inches through a channel in the centers of the vertebrae. And branching off from the cord, from the big bundle of nerves, nerve roots emerge between the vertebrae—one pair of nerve roots (one for each side of the body) coming out between one pair of vertebrae, until all told 31 pairs of spinal nerves fan out, each serving a particular body area.

In emerging from the cord, a nerve root passes through a foramen, a hole formed between two vertebrae to allow the passage. Such is the geographic relationship of disk to foramen that if the disk should herniate, its extruded portion can compress a nerve root against the bony wall of the foramen.

Injury to the tough outer covering of the disk may occur gradually over many years—as the result, for example, of almost constant jarring activity. Or it may occur suddenly as the result of a very bad fall or other serious accident. With sufficient injury to the disk covering, the gelatinous central nucleus pulposus of the disk may pour out much like toothpaste from a tube when the tube develops a small hole. If the nucleus pulposus is extruded at a site where it presses upon a nerve root, there will be pain. If the material later breaks off so that pressure is relieved, the pain will disappear, some say.

The disk most likely to become herniated is the one at the lumbosacral junction, between the fifth, or lowest, lumbar vertebra and the first sacral vertebra. Here, there is greatest motion in the forward-and-back (anteroposterior) plane. Recall that the sacral vertebrae are fused; there can be no individual motion for them. But the lumbar vertebrae can move, and at the lumbosacral junction a lot of motion is concentrated.

Depending upon the location of a damaged disk and the nerve roots involved, one or more areas of the body may become painful. Most often, however, because it is the disk between the fifth lumbar and first sacral vertebra that herniates,

pain will be felt along the course of the sciatic nerve—down the back of the thigh and usually into the side of the foot. Nearly always one leg or the other is affected. If, in a rare case, the disk herniates exactly in the midline and the extrusion of nucleus is great enough, there may be pressure on both of the pair of nerves and both legs may be involved.

With a herniated disk, the mere act of walking, especially on a hard surface, can produce great discomfort. Sneezing, coughing, and other quick movements often aggravate the pain to an excruciating level.

Actually, low back pain is a relatively small and later accompaniment of the leg pain which is most characteristic of disk herniation. Usually, the leg pain comes first; it may be followed by "pins and needles" sensations, numbness, and weakness of the leg; then may come low back pain and muscle spasm; still later atrophy, or wasting, of the leg may develop.

PSEUDODISK OR "PINCHED NERVE" PAIN

Typical sciatica—or down-the-leg pain—may result from causes other than a herniated intervertebral disk.

It makes no difference where a nerve is compressed or pinched—at the point where it emerges from the spinal cord, at its terminus far away, or anywhere in between—wherever it is put under pressure, the pressure can produce sciatica.

Not infrequently, sciatica much like that stemming from a herniated disk—and mistaken by its victim for that—arises when a muscle in spasm, contracted abnormally, puts pressure on the nerve. Sometimes, the nerve may be squeezed between two muscles, both of which are in spasm.

Physicians often refer to sciatica arising from a cause other than herniated disk as "pseudodisk" syndrome.

SPRAINS AND STRAINS

Muscles are tough. So are the ligaments, the flexible bands of connective tissue connecting bones where they join in joints; so, too, the tendons ("gristle") which attach muscles to bones.

But any of these structures anywhere in the body can be injured, and those in the back are certainly not immune. An injurious force can strain a muscle, ligament or tendon, pulling it beyond normal limits. There may then be some immediate pain in the back, which disappears after a time, and if the strain has been mild, that is the end of the incident.

With more severe strain, an inflammatory reaction often develops, leading to fluid collection in the tissues. As the tissues become congested with the fluid, pressure may build up on nerve endings, and pain results. When fluid collects in muscles, there is stiffness, and the day after the injury the stiffness may increase and pain may develop. This is a typical pattern, for example, whenever you put to sudden vigorous use muscles not accustomed to such activity. If you haven't done so for a long time and ride a horse, row a boat, play a set of tennis, chop wood, shovel snow, etc., etc., you can expect to be stiff and sore the next day, victim of a "charleyhorse."

When a structure in the back is strained, the pain is likely to be diffuse. Pain tends to be less localized in the back than in other regions of the body. If you are blindfolded, and somebody holds two pin points just a fraction of an inch apart and touches them to various parts of your body, you will, in many areas, be able to tell that you are being touched with two points (rather than one) but not necessarily when they are touched to the back.

With a strain in the back, there may be some disturbance of normal motion in addition to pain, but usually movement is not greatly affected, and gradually the strain will be repaired and its effects will disappear.

A sprain is another matter.

While strain involves only stretching, a sprain is a more severe injury involving a partial tear, sometimes even a complete tear, in a ligament, tendon, or muscle. The tissue reaction to the more severe injury is much quicker than to a strain. The tissues become engorged with fluid and also with blood coming from torn blood vessels, and there is immediate severe pain.

Sometimes, the injurious force capable of producing a sprain may be directed in such a way that a ligament or tendon is not itself torn but instead pulls away a tip of bone. This is known as an avulsion fracture, and the effect is much the same as a tear in the ligament or tendon.

When large muscles or ligaments of the back are sprained, the pain may be widespread. And when severe sprain affects small muscles or ligaments which ordinarily help stabilize the spinal column, pain may spread as other muscles try to compensate and, in doing so, painfully overcontract. Moreover, since these would-be-helpful muscles do not necessarily pull in exactly the same direction as the injured muscle or muscles, their hard work may be futile. Still other muscles then may try to help and painfully overcontract. In some cases, as the result of efforts of other muscles to compensate, the back may even list to one side. The tilt is called functional scoliosis.

If it happens that a ligament surrounding an intervertebral disk is severely sprained, the disk may herniate and the forced-out or extruded nucleus pulposus material of the disk may put pressure on a nerve.

People who have experienced sprains and fractures anywhere in the body know that it is not unusual for the pain of a fracture to disappear long before the pain of a sprain. A sprain, in fact, may be painful for a year or more if healing should be retarded because of undue stretching of the healing areas of the torn fibers.

The body has its intrinsic repair processes. With a strain, the mild damage produces mild inflammation. Gradually the inflammation fluid is absorbed, and when that happens there is virtually no damage left. For a strain, anything that helps increase blood supply to the area, and thus speeds the absorption of the fluid, is useful. Mild heat and gentle motion may be all that are needed.

When sprain produces a tear, healing must take place. It does—through the formation of fibrous, or scar, tissue. Whereas tissue in a ligament or tendon is often elastic, fibrous tissue does not have the same degree of elasticity but it is strong repair stuff. A muscle tear is also repaired with fibrous tissue, and although the healed area does not have the ability of muscle tissue to contract, it holds together the muscle so that the rest of it can then carry out the contracting function.

Muscle tears—because muscles have a rich supply of blood to nourish them and bring in repair materials at a rapid rate—heal much more quickly than do tears of ligaments and tendons, which lack a rich blood supply; but, given time, ligaments and tendons heal.

The torn ligament of a disk can also heal with time. Here again, the healing involves formation of fibrous tissue. If the nucleus pulposus of the disk has not pushed out in such a way as to put pressure on a nerve root, there will be no sciatica or leg pain, only back pain from the sprained ligament; and with the healing of the ligament, the pain may disappear.

It is worth noting about disk herniation that it often may cause an inflammatory reaction which is only temporary but may be more significant than the pressure of the protruding nucleus pulposus in producing pain. The protruding portion of nucleus sometimes will pinch off and drop down in the dural sac, the baglike membrane that surrounds the nervous system and contains a protective cushioning fluid, where it is of no consequence. Moreover, quite often, the nucleus may return to its normal position within a disk if squeezing pressure on it can be reduced, and this is often possible with rest and measures to overcome muscle spasm. Meanwhile, whether the once-protruding nucleus has dropped off or returned to its normal position within the disk, the pressure it may have put upon a nerve root may have produced an inflammatory reaction, swelling the nerve root and causing pain. In that case, when the inflammation subsides, as it almost invariably does once the cause of it is no longer present, the pain will disappear.

ARTHRITIC CHANGES

The joints of the spine, like joints elsewhere in the body, may be affected by arthritis—arthritis of any of many types, ranging from infectious to rheumatoid.

With rheumatoid and other inflammatory types of arthritis, joint tissues become swollen, boggy, and painful. Much more common, however, is another type of arthritis—osteoarthritis, or, as it is sometimes called, "wear-and-tear" arthritis.

To some extent, all of us are subject to osteoarthritis. A certain degree of wear and tear is inevitable. In youth, repair processes keep up with the wear and tear. As we get older, the repair processes may slow somewhat while the destructive processes continue as before or even become accentuated. Such accentuation can come from many influences.

The medical author recalls an interesting experience he had while serving with the Air Force in California. Quite a few children were found to be suffering severe osteoarthritis of the knees. There was some mystery about this—until an investigation established that the wear and tear in the knee joints was being caused by participation in a popular sport of the time, racing small, high-speed boats in irrigation canals. Boys would kneel in the boats and be bounced up and down, and the bouncing produced excessive wear of the knee joints. Commonly, the knees of obese people are more affected by osteoarthritis than those of people of normal weight because the greater weight burden produces more wear and tear.

Joints in the spine also may be affected by osteoarthritis because of excess weight, poor posture, and weak musculature, any and all of which can put an abnormal burden on the joints. People with scoliosis, or bending of the spine—whether the scoliosis was present at birth or developed from injury, disease, or poor posture—have increased stress on back joints on one side or the other. Whenever undue pressure is long-continued on one side of a joint because the joint is not aligned properly, the side experiencing the greater pressure is subject to increased wear and tear which can result in pain.

The pain, moreover, may occur in more than one place because of the back's efforts at compensation. For example, the individual who habitually slumps forward and becomes round-shouldered may develop pain not only in the upper back but also in the low back because of a compensatory excessive curvature in the low back—lordosis or swayback—which leads to excessive strain and wear and tear in the lower joints.

THE SPINE-BENDING MECHANISM

A discussion of what happens in scoliosis can be helpful in understanding not only the back pain associated with that condition but back pain in general.

Bone appears to be similar to a piezoelectric crystal—a crystal so named because, when bent or stressed, it produces a small electric current. It is such a current in bone that calls for the production of new bone and orients the direction in which the new bone is laid down.

Actually, it has become possible recently to stimulate bone growth—and even the healing of fractures—by the application of small electric currents. Moreover, both orthodontic treatment (in which braces are applied to the teeth to help straighten them) and orthopedic treatment (in which splints and braces may be used to help correct clubfeet, scoliosis, and other bone deformities in a growing child) are based on the principle of applying controlled stress so as to produce electric currents in bone and further the laying down of new bone in one direction rather than another.

Related to this is another phenomenon associated with connective tissue, which is the primary stuff of ligaments and tendons. Muscles are contractile and exert pull; they pull on tendons. Connective tissue, when allowed to relax, tends to shrink. As long as stretching and shrinking are alternated, tendons and ligaments tend to remain at their normal length. (People who want to be limber know they must regularly carry out movements which stretch ligaments and tendons; otherwise they become stiff.)

Any time a joint in a normal individual is maintained for a prolonged period in one position, the connective tissues on the concave side, or inside curve, of the joint will shorten while those on the convex side will stretch. With stretching of connective tissues, there is some weakening of muscles.

So rapidly do connective tissues tend to contract if not used that it is not uncommon, for example, for a person who fractures a wrist and must wear a cast, extending to and above the elbow, until the wrist heals to experience elbow stiffness and to require an exercise program to restore flexibility to the elbow even though it was not hurt originally.

Much the same thing happens to the person with a swayback. Abdominal muscles are weak and since there is excessive lordosis, the connective tissues in the back of the spine shorten while those in front are stretched. The abdomen becomes protuberant. Pressure on the spinal joints is no longer distributed equally, and where it is excessive there may be excessive wear and tear.

And in scoliosis, once abnormal curvature begins to develop in a growing spine, gravity pulls on neck, arms, and upper trunk, thus tending to increase the curvature. At first, the curvature may be readily reversible. But after a time, the connective tissues on the concave sides of the joints contract. If correction is not instituted at this point, then, with long-continued greater pressure on one side of bone than on the other side, bone will grow more on the convex side of the curve where pressure is less and may stop growing or even begin to resorb or dis-appear on the concave side where pressure is greater. The bones then become relatively wedge-shaped instead of relatively square as viewed from the front. Once such bone changes occur, correction requires measures to reverse the forces or pressures on the bones so they will now grow more rapidly on the side that was concave.

FRACTURES

Bone anywhere in the body may on occasion be fractured. The most common fracture in the spinal column is the compression fracture of a vertebral body, in which the body is compressed mostly in front.

Once the fracture itself was the focus of medical attention. It could be seen readily on x-rays. What could not be seen was the associated damage to soft tissues—muscles, ligaments, and tendons.

Now it is recognized that the stress on soft tissues before the fracture or crushing of bone actually takes place may be the significant factor in back pain. Actually, many people have been found, on x-ray examinations, to have compressed vertebrae although they had never been aware of any pain or of any incident that might have led to the compression. Fortunately, in their cases, soft-tissue injuries were slight.

A sizable proportion of compression fractures occur in the upper lumbar and dorsal regions of the spine. But it often happens that soft tissues at lower levels of the spine are placed under great stress and may be injured, too, before the fracture develops higher up.

Today, in the case of a compression fracture, the medical effort is largely concentrated on rehabilitating the affected muscles, ligaments, and tendons to relieve pain and derangement.

PINCHED FAT

Another possible cause of back pain is pinched fat tissue.

Fat is laid down in the body in characteristic patterns, separated usually by layers of connective tissue called fascia. The fat is just below the skin as well as deeper. If a small perforation or hole should develop in a fascial layer because of injury, a small globule of fat may push its way through the hole when the hole is stretched; and when the patient relaxes so that the hole is no longer stretched, the fat globule may be caught in the hole, pinched, and may then become painful.

Injection of cortisone to help reduce inflammation may be enough to end the pain. In rare cases, the hole in the fascial layer may have to be enlarged surgically to end the pinching of fat. There is usually no need to remove the globule itself unless the pinching has so interfered with blood supply that the fat has become a hard lump of dead tissue.

CONGENITAL DEFECTS

Backs are as varied as people. While no two backs are exactly alike, the differences usually are relatively minor ones. But major differences—abnormalities present at birth—do occur and may take many forms.

Sometimes back pain is associated with a congenital abnormality but is not due to the abnormality itself. Rather, the pain stems from unusual stresses imposed by the abnormality on surrounding structures, especially the muscles. In such cases, surgery may be required to correct the abnormality. Often, without recourse to surgery, braces and corsets may be helpful. And a conservative method of treatment that frequently is of great benefit involves exercises to strengthen those muscles that can be used to counter the pain-producing effects of the unusual stress.

THE SHORT LEG

Slight variation in length of the legs is not unusual. In most cases, a difference of as much as half an inch causes no problems. But a greater difference—and, on occasion, even a lesser one—may be a contributing factor in back pain because of the unusual stress it places on back structures.

Moreover, it is possible to have a "short leg effect," with painful stress on back structures, although there is no actual anatomical difference in leg length. That is because in walking the legs go through various motions including shortening. The shortening is achieved through flexion at the hips, knees, and ankles. If there should be some difference between the legs in the degree of flexion at hip, knee, or ankle, then, for all practical purposes, there may be a functional, even though not an anatomical, difference in leg length.

We will have more to say about leg length and the short leg effect later.

A VARIETY OF POSSIBLE NONLOCAL CAUSES

Back pain can result from conditions that have nothing to do with the back itself. Heart disease sometimes may produce back pain. So, on occasion, may disease of the lungs, diaphragm, abdomen, kidney, uterus, ovaries, fallopian tubes, or prostate.

Pain can radiate. It may originate at one site and, through

circuitous nerve pathways, fan out and produce pain at distant sites. It sometimes happens that the only pain produced by peptic ulcer, colitis, or gallbladder disease is back pain.

Women sometimes have pain referred to the back because of menstrual disturbances, pregnancy, pelvic congestion, pelvic displacement, and even because of ill-fitting diaphragms or pessaries.

MAJOR CAUSE: MUSCLES

Despite the many possible causes of backache, some of them subtle and insidious, the problem in the great majority of backaches lies with muscles, muscles in the abdomen as well as in the back itself: muscles that are weak, unable to perform properly, easily subject to injury.

Few of us are aware of the vital importance of muscles, both for overall health and for health of the back. Bones, of course, form the framework of the body, joints permit movement, and muscles do the moving. The hundreds of voluntary muscles in the human body which control everyday movements weigh 250 percent as much as all bones together. Beyond movement, muscles provide the means of communication—through talking, writing, facial expression.

It is largely how much muscles are used and how many calories are burned up in their use that determine whether body weight remains constant and healthy or becomes excessive. It is muscle use that helps to determine whether healthy blood circulation is maintained—for one thing, because the use of leg muscles helps to pump blood in the leg veins back toward the heart. And the health of the heart itself is determined to no small extent by muscular activity, for it is such activity that trains the heart, itself a muscle, to beat more efficiently. There is evidence, too, that physical activity is a factor of importance in helping to maintain normal levels of cholesterol and other fats in the blood and in preventing their accumulation on artery walls with such ultimately crippling or lethal results as strokes and heart attacks.

And muscles are critically important for the back.

The spinal column, as already noted, is an S-shaped column of bones, with disks between for cushioning, and with ligaments to hold the bones and disks somewhat loosely and flexibly. Muscles must provide the major support for the column, keeping it erect, and bending and turning it.

When man assumed an upright posture, muscles—abdominal and hip muscles as well as those in the back—had to take on the job of supporting the spinal column.

Inherently, they have the capacity for the job. Muscle tissue is formed before birth, and the muscle fiber supply we are born with is ours for life. The fibers, of course, grow as the rest of the body does during childhood and adolescence. There are some 6 trillion muscle fibers making up the muscles of the human body. Each fiber is about the size of a hair, yet it is capable of supporting 1,000 times its own weight.

Muscle strength develops as fibers contract, contract, contract. Strength is maintained and muscles remain in good condition only when used. If they fall into some disuse, they only weaken; if they fall into complete disuse, they may actually atrophy or waste away, as demonstrated in paralyzed patients whose muscles waste unless passive exercises are used to keep them moving.

In our increasingly sedentary way of life, unless we take special precautions, our muscles become victimized by disuse. They have less bulk, become flabby, are not capable of vigorous or sustained activity; any unusual exertion puts a strain on them with resulting pain.

One famed study, by Dr. Hardin Jones of the University of California, has shown graphically the effects of sedentary living on muscles. The study made use of the fact that when muscles are exercised little or not at all, they have less need for blood and nourishment. As a result, many if not most of the capillaries, the tiniest blood vessels, which supply them collapse; they are unneeded. Jones used special instrumentation to measure blood flow through the muscles of teen-agers and of men of various ages. He established that from age 18 to age 25, the flow drops by 40 percent; by age 35, it is down 60 percent. In terms of circulation for muscles, the average sedentary American man is middle-aged by the time he is 26, and by age 35 he is, in terms of both muscle circulation and sense of physical vigor, less than half the man he used to be.

Not only can strong muscles provide the support a normal back requires; they may even do much to compensate for any serious damage to back structures. One of many cases in point is the fencing instructor mentioned in Chapter 1 who, despite severe degeneration of virtually all his intervertebral disks and with severe arthritis in addition, could remain vigorously active and less subject to frequent, severe backaches than many people free of disk problems and other organic back disorders.

The deterioration of muscular fitness in an increasingly sedentary society accounts for a markedly increasing predisposition to back pain. Nor is it a matter only of back muscle deterioration—a fact that deserves repeated emphasis.

Consider a tree or a telephone pole held erect by four guy wires so it is stable even in high winds. If one of the wires is cut, the tree or pole may fall, and it will fall in the direction of an uncut wire.

That situation is only partially analogous to what happens in a human with weak stomach muscles. In theory, perhaps, such a person's back should fall backward, since there is no guying or support from in front. But this does not happen because we have a sense of balance which assures that we will maintain our center of gravity above our feet. So, to compensate for weak abdominal muscles, we shift body weight, leaning slightly forward, hanging on our back muscles since they are the stronger guy wires.

But this has a deleterious effect, placing continuous excess strain on the back muscles. After a time, they fatigue and hurt. And in our society, weakness of abdominal muscles is one of the most common causes of back pain. One study at the State University of Iowa College of Medicine found that in chronic backache patients, abdominal muscles often are *less than one third* as strong as back muscles—and, in that study and others, very often strengthening of abdominal muscles proved to be all that was necessary to eliminate backaches.

An additional result of muscle disuse is loss of elasticity. The contractile elements of unused muscles tend to stay in shortened position, and protein is laid down around the fibers and in and around the joints, producing contractures which tend to limit joint motion. Attempts then to move the back through the normal range of motion may cause tugging on the contractures around the spinal joints, with resulting pain.

Almost invariably, if people with back pain put any blame at all on muscles, they indict the back muscles. On the surface, it seems logical since the pain is in the back. But it's there because the weakness of stomach or hip muscles or both has put an intolerable load on the back muscles.

Sprains and strains are common when tired or weak muscles are called upon suddenly to do more than they are capable of doing. Nor is this a matter only of unusual exertion such as shoveling snow or lifting a very heavy load; even a sudden coughing spell may be enough to produce damage.

SPASM

The immediate cause of acute pain in most backaches is spasm, an involuntary sustained contraction of muscle. In a way, spasm is a protective mechanism. If a joint, for example, is injured, muscles about the joint contract and stay contracted, serving as a kind of protective splint for the injured joint. If a muscle is injured or is under excessive strain, it may go into spasm, and other nearby muscles may do the same in an effort to splint the strained muscle and prevent further damage to it.

But spasm can be extremely painful. While muscle is not tender in its normal state and can be pressed upon and kneaded without pain, it becomes tender and painful when it is swollen by the constant tension of spasm.

The pain of spasm results from lack of nutrition. In muscle, as elsewhere in the body, blood with its oxygen and nutrients comes in through arteries and then, carrying a load of waste products of metabolism from the muscle cells, leaves through veins. It is through thin-walled capillaries, tiny vessels lying between arteries and veins, that oxygen and nutrients move from blood to muscle cells, and in turn metabolic wastes move from cells to blood.

When muscle contracts, the capillaries are squeezed shut. Ordinarily, the contraction is over quickly and the exchange of materials can take place normally. But if a muscle stays in contraction—in spasm—oxygen and food cannot reach the muscle cells and waste products cannot be removed. The waste products, which include lactic acid, can produce pain when they accumulate in muscle. Lactic acid in excess is a notable irritant of nerve endings. Moreover a muscle in spasm is working, since it is contracting; and the lack of oxygen causes the muscle tissues to cry out in pain.

SPASM AND EMOTIONAL TENSION

Muscle spasm can be triggered by injury or excessive demand—and it can also be induced by emotional tension.

Muscle tension is a normal biological response to emotional

tension. The most common of all headaches, for example, is the tension headache characterized by muscle pain in the neck and back of the head. It occurs because the muscles are held in constant tension, leading to obstruction of blood flow and buildup of lactic acid. One indication of the involvement of emotions in tension headaches is that most victims get only mild or moderate relief from aspirin or other analgesics and, for optimal benefit, require relief of their emotional tension through sedatives or other measures.

Emotions often play a significant role in back pain. Man, along with all animals, is endowed with ability to respond to emergencies. Elaborate mechanisms make it possible to fight or flee for protection. When confronted by a situation that represents a threat of some kind, many body systems are affected: glands and their hormone outpourings, the blood pressure regulatory system, the breathing regulatory system—and, most important, the muscles.

Muscles, of course, are used for fleeing, fighting, even posturing. A frightened cat, for example, bristles its hair, tightens its skin, and arches its back; it paws an attacking object or, if the fright is sufficient, runs away.

Unfortunately, civilized man in many instances can neither fight nor flee. His body is prepared for physical action of some kind but he takes none, of the fighting or fleeing kind. Angry and yet thinking better of expressing the anger, he may grit his teeth, using facial muscles for the purpose; enough such gritting may cause jaw pain. As anger rises, he may hunch up his shoulders, using muscles of the neck and the back; and constant tension of these muscles can cause pain in the neck and the back and in a tight band around the head because the muscles pull on the skull's covering layers.

Emotional tension, enough in itself sometimes to initiate spasm and pain, is often a compounding influence. It may bar muscular relaxation, and a muscle must relax to be able to maintain healthy function. Over a period of time, a chronically tensed muscle may lose its stretch and become shortened. This, in itself, may induce painful conditions. It may also lead to awkward, jerky movements which may make the muscle more susceptible to injury.

Life, of course, is full of irritations. We live in an increasingly noisy, crowded world. Traffic jams are not soothing, nor the cacophony of automobile horns, nor the jostling in crowds. It is certainly not entirely abnormal to seethe to some extent when irritated, although some of us seethe much more than others. It is difficult to avoid becoming emotionally tense when confronted with family problems, job problems, financial problems.

But if emotional tension cannot be entirely avoided, muscle tension need not inevitably follow. Physical activity requires muscles to move, and because muscles generally work against each other, one going into relaxation as the other contracts, and then vice versa, activity helps to achieve muscle relaxation.

Exercise also provides an outlet for the body energy mustered by emotional tension. The aroused person, unable to fight or flee, does a healthy thing in exercising away the emergency forces his body has developed. The exercising helps to dissipate both the emotional tension and the muscle tension.

DIFFERING REACTIONS TO PAIN

People vary greatly in their reactions to pain—so much so that there has even grown up a rigid set of commonly held convictions about how different groups react. But recent scientific investigations suggest that as often as not the convictions may be faulty, based on myths or very limited observations.

For example, one recent large-scale study would seem to debunk three long-standing notions: (1) that older people tolerate pain better than younger people; (2) that women can tolerate more pain than men; and (3) that nonwhite peoples are far more tolerant of pain than whites.

The year-long study covered 41,000 Californians who took a pain test as part of a regular physical checkup given to members of the Kaiser-Permanente group health plan. Told only that they were taking a "pressure tolerance" test, the subjects placed their heels in a viselike machine and were asked to try to stand the pressure as long as possible. Plastic-tipped metal rods squeezed the Achilles tendon in the heel, applying pressure that could increase up to a level of 50 pounds per square inch.

Sure enough, there were clear differences in pain tolerance levels, according to age, sex, and race. But contrary to the popular notion, women on the average were able to bear only half as much pain as men. Both men and women showed a steady decrease in tolerance with age; men over 60, for example, could take less than 75 percent of the pain that men in their 20's could take. Racial differences were not quite as distinct, but there were indications that whites may have greater pain tolerance than blacks and that Orientals, often thought of as particularly stoic, may have the lowest tolerance of all.

One possible shortcoming of the California test, and of other studies of a similar nature, may be the inability to measure emotional elements.

Emotional elements have much to do with pain tolerance as well as pain causation. Physicians have long been aware, as a matter of simple observation, that the worry accompanying a serious illness can increase a patient's sensation of pain beyond the pain actually engendered by the physical source.

In the same person, pain tolerance varies with mood swings; the same level of pain that may be acceptable at one moment may be intolerable at another.

It is sometimes claimed that many job-connected back pains are really much less painful than their victims make out, that malingering (the feigning of severe pain) is very common.

Undoubtedly, there are instances of malingering but more often, in our experience, there is no conscious effort to defraud; instead, a complaint that should be relatively minor on physical grounds alone has become major because of emotional stress.

In only a handful of many thousands of cases seen at ICD has the patient appeared to be making a conscious effort to defraud the employer or an insurance firm. When a patient's pain is out of proportion to what it should be on the basis of physicial condition, it is usually for understandable emotional reasons. Many patients are terrified about what their complaint may mean for their future and the future of their families. Often they are worried and confused for lack of adequate explanation of what has happened to them, what can be done about it, and what the outcome is likely to be.

A man approaching middle age may come to think that half his life is gone and that he is, to some extent, over the hill and on the downhill side. He feels that his physical prowess is reduced, his sexual ability diminished, his thinking processes slower than in youth. When he has the additional trauma of back pain, he may need repeated reassurance that he will not inevitably lose his job nor have his self-esteem further threatened by inability to meet the demands of family life, sexual as well as economic.

Women, too, may experience some emotional trauma as they approach menopause, feeling themselves to be "less woman." When back pain which may inhibit sexual activities is superimposed, their self-confidence may be further shaken. We have seen many examples of this.

CHAPTER 3

YOUR OWN TESTS

AND CHECKS FOR

COMMON CAUSES

While the possible causes of backaches are many, the probable are relatively few. The chances are excellent that you can establish, with relative ease and quite quickly, what is behind your pain episodes.

Some of the tests that may be required for the comparatively rare causes of backache can be complex, requiring both special equipment and long diagnostic experience. But the tests that very often can pick out common causes are simple in principle and require no special ability. You will be able to carry out many of the tests yourself; for some, you will need help from a family member or a friend—brief help—and you will have no difficulty indicating to him or her what has to be done.

HOW TO CHECK FOR SPASM

Muscle spasm, as we have indicated, is a common denominator in most backaches and means continued, involuntary contraction of muscle. If you've ever experienced an eye tic, for example, you are aware of one form of spasm, usually quite minor.

Spasm, if long-continued, may lead to muscle tenderness, and the muscle will be painful when pressed upon. With severe spasm, pain may be present even without pressure. The muscle also may be hard and knotty, with its motion markedly restricted. With severe spasm of a neck muscle, for example, it may be impossible to bend the neck enough to bring an ear close to a shoulder or to place the chin on a shoulder.

But even when severe, all spasm is not necessarily obvious. If several muscles go into spasm, only the most painful will be noted. It's as if the brain must be aware of, and attend fully only to, the most disturbing of disturbances; one thing at a time, and that one the most demanding. Once the pain of the most painful muscle is overcome, that of the next most painful will be felt. In effect, there is a hierarchy of pain appreciation. Because of this, one must not assume that spasm is limited to an area in which pain is felt; there may be need to check elsewhere for it as well.

Since it is virtually impossible for anyone to reach all over his own back to check for muscles in spasm, you will need a friend or family member to help. Have him check with the heel of his hand or his fingertips.

The fingertips are more sensitive but if not properly used may elicit more pain when a spasm area is reached. The correct procedure is to place the fingertips of one hand directly on the body and the fingertips of the second hand on top of those of the first. Press down with the fingertips of the second hand, not those of the first.

With either fingertips or heel of the hand, the motion used should be gentle, somewhat like that employed for kneading dough for bread or pastry. When a muscle is not in spasm, it can be pushed, lifted and wiggled over underlying bone without pain. If such maneuvers produce pain, or if there is tender-

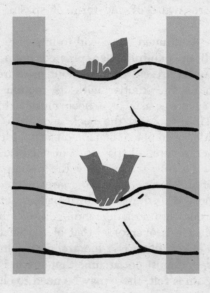

ness when the examiner's hand is applied gently, that particular muscle is in spasm.

Spasm may be more difficult to evaluate in people who are emotionally tense and tend to keep their muscles tensed, so that they may not be readily maneuvered by an examiner. There are also people who, with or without being emotionally tense, are not as adept as others in relaxing muscles at will. In medicine, we sometimes call such people "muscle morons," and the term is not meant to be generally derogatory or to reflect on intelligence. It simply means that such people have low muscle-control capability as compared with the general run of people; at the other extreme are some athletes and all belly-dancers and burlesque house queens who can make individual muscles do their bidding with startling effects.

When muscles are taut because the individual holds them that way rather than because they are in spasm, they will usually not be tender, or any tenderness present will be very mild.

Often, it is possible for the examiner to induce relaxation. When, for example, the complaint is upper back or neck pain, he can gently move the patient's head from side to side and forward and back until the patient relaxes and muscles in the area loosen. It may take patience but often such relaxation can be achieved; and when it is, the area of muscle spasm can be located more readily.

There are measures that can be used to induce relaxation when the problem is low in the back. With the patient lying prone, the buttocks should feel soft and doughy, and should be easily indentable when fingertip pressure is applied. If they are not, then the patient is holding the buttock muscles contracted. It often helps if the patient tries, alternately, to contract and relax those muscles so that he becomes more aware of when they are relaxed and may then be able to keep them relaxed.

If this does not work, the examiner can use a gentle clapping massage, with palms of the hands held cuplike and rapidly, but gently, pounded on the buttocks. Sometimes, even more effective is a massage maneuver in which the hands are held in the vertical position, thumbs up, and their bottom edges are used to gently and rapidly percuss the buttocks.

Still another measure that may be helpful in inducing relaxation is to have the patient lie prone or supine on a bed while the examiner gently raises his arms or legs and lets them drop gently from a height of one or two inches. Dropping them from greater heights should be avoided, since the patient may fear injury and tense up even more.

For some people, pleasant mental images are aids to achieving muscle relaxation. Asked to think of a situation they find attractive—perhaps sitting contentedly in a boat with a fishing line over the side, or sitting half-asleep in the sunshine, or lying in the warm sand on a beach—many people can let go physically.

There are a few patients, we have found, who can relax only when asked to do exactly the opposite of what the examiner really wants them to do or what they are already doing. Thus, for example, if the need is to relax the back muscles, it may help to have the patient lie on one side, bend forward, and then try to relax. When he fails to relax completely and remains partially bent forward, he will—willy-nilly, in that position—have relaxed his back muscles.

Muscle spasm should be evaluated before using any measures aimed at relieving the back pain and should be reevaluated after their use. (The relief measures—which include hot baths, counterirritants, muscle relaxants, analgesics—are discussed in detail in later chapters.) It is important to test before and after in order to determine, beyond relief of pain, just how much relief of spasm has been achieved. Relieving spasm is therapeutic and often aids diagnosis as well—for if a trigger point is involved in producing the spasm and pain, the trigger point may be difficult or impossible to locate until the spasm is relieved.

So, after the first important home diagnostic check for spasm and after its relief, the next should be for the presence of any trigger points.

HOW TO LOCATE TRIGGER POINTS

A trigger point is a small area, generally so circumscribed that you can cover the whole of it with a fingertip. Any area of tenderness that is larger than that usually indicates either muscle spasm surrounding a trigger point or muscle spasm alone. You can locate a trigger point with a fingertip; the area will be tender or even quite painful; and if you move the fingertip even just half an inch, it will then be over a much less painful or even pain-free area.

By exploring over the back for such small areas of special tenderness or pain—helped by a friend or family member—you should be able to determine whether any trigger points are present.

Trigger points have sometimes been biopsied during surgery, and the little removed sections of tissue have been sent to the laboratory for microscopic study. Some such studies have found evidence of chronic inflammatory cells, but others have revealed nothing unusual. Electrical testing has shown nothing unusual about trigger points.

But while we are not certain about what a trigger point is, we do know that it is more than spasm. Spasm is less localized. Spasm can be a reaction to irritation of a trigger point—i.e., a secondary effect. Muscle spasm may develop without a trigger point. It may follow exposure to a cold draft, extreme exertion, unusual emotional tension. On the other hand, these same conditions may cause formation of trigger points. It sometimes happens that spasm follows when a trigger point is moved during muscle contraction so that the sequence of events may be (1) draft, exertion, or emotional tension; (2) trigger point development; (3) muscle spasm.

It is important to find any trigger points because treatment for them differs from treatment for spasm. While spasm may be relieved by such measures as heat, cold, massage, counterirritants, trigger points may require injection or needling.

TIGHTNESS

A common reason for pain is pull upon tight structures. Thus, anyone with tight hamstring muscles (which run from the lower buttocks along the thighs to just below the knees) or tight back muscles will experience pain during an attempt to touch the floor while keeping the knees straight. The pain will be in the back if tight back muscles are pulled upon, or will be in the buttock, back of the thigh and perhaps behind the knee when the hamstrings are tight.

A first test for tightness of the hamstring and back muscles is, in fact, an effort to touch the floor with knees straight—but in a specific way. A common error is to try to force or "bounce" oneself down to floor-touching—to lean forward and bounce down and up. The result may be severe pain. Instead, one should bend the neck and head gently, and then, in relaxed manner, let the arms droop forward toward the floor and bend slowly as far as possible. One should then estimate, or have someone measure, the distance between fingertips and floor and record this for future use in evaluating progress in improving the elasticity and flexibility of the muscles, tendons, and joints.

Failure to touch the floor indicates that one or both muscle groups—back and hamstring—may be tight. To determine which, other tests can be used.

Hamstring tightness is best tested for with the help of someone to perform a few simple movements. Sit erect on the edge of a table with back arched so there is a hollow in the low back, the normal lordotic position. Hold the edge of the table with your hands. The legs should be dangling and the person helping you should then lift each lower leg and straighten the knee slowly and gently while you sit erect. If he is unable to straighten the knees without forcing you to bend your back or lean backward, then your hamstring muscles are excessively tight, and you should take measures, to be discussed later, to make them more elastic.

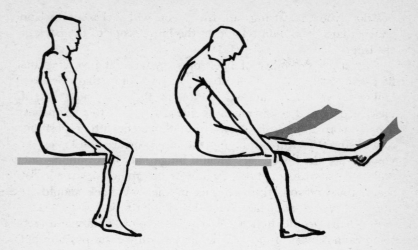

If you have no one to help you, you can make use of another method of testing for hamstring tightness. Stand with knees straight and hands behind your back, with the backs of the hands facing but not actually touching the buttocks. Your chin should be forward and your neck arched upward toward the ceiling. Gently lower your body until, if possible, your trunk forms a 90-degree angle with your thighs. Your face should be pointed forward. If you are unable to bend to the 90-degree

position, your hamstrings are tight. You will feel some tension and perhaps even pain related to the buttocks or to the back of the thighs.

To test for flexibility of back muscles without involving the hamstrings, sit erect. As you do so, you will notice that there is a hollow in the back, an indentation in the low back that, if measured, would be as much as one and a half to two inches. This is normal lordosis. Now, from the erect sitting position, slowly slump forward, bringing the chest toward the knees. As you do this, the lower back should bulge out. This bulging out, or kyphosis, with forward bending of the spine is normal. For the normal person, the kyphosis in the low back should be about one third to one half as much as the lordosis.

But many people do not have that degree of kyphosis; in fact, some cannot even bring the low back to fully erect position but maintain it constantly in the lordotic position.

It can be important to differentiate between tightness of hamstring and back muscles because some people are able to touch fingertips to the floor from a standing position by overutilizing the lumbar spine and underutilizing the hamstring muscles. They are able to move their spine beyond normal and in so doing make up for tight hamstrings, but this may be a cause of back pain, since the joints may be damaged by the abnormal motion.

A CHECK ON POSTURE

Some degree of lordosis of the lumbar spine in the low back is normal. But excessive lordosis is a frequent cause of back pain and is commonly associated with another most frequent cause: weak abdominal muscles.

A typical back-pain patient has weak abdominal muscles,

protuberant abdomen, hyperlordosis with swayback, and tight hamstrings.

In checking posture, the total body profile should be looked at in a mirror with an unprejudiced eye. Do not make any effort to stand more erect than usual. Stand in a normal relaxed position. (It is important not to try to assume a military posture since this is abnormal and, if maintained for a prolonged period, can cause pain.)

Just remember that you are testing yourself and not trying to kid yourself.

Hyperlordosis with deep swayback often is quite obvious in the mirror. But in the heavy or extremely muscular person with a thick fat or muscular padding over the spine, it may not be apparent. Sometimes, in such people, hyperlordosis may have to be inferred from the protuberant abdomen and excessive kyphosis of the upper trunk which almost invariably accompany hyperlordosis.

Good posture is often mistakenly considered to be an unvarying, ramrod-stiff bearing. Any such "ideal" posture is not natural and can be maintained only for a short period. In fact, no posture is normally maintained for any length of time. We constantly shift from one posture to another, to provide relief for muscles which have to work in maintaining position. When we sit, we do not sit still; when we lie down, we do not lie still—as witness the wrinkling and disarray of bed linens in the morning. Twisting and turning even during sleep is a protective mechanism, for pressure on any part of the body cannot be maintained for long before blood flow to the area is impeded as the pressure constricts the capillaries, the tiny blood vessels through which tissues receive nourishment from the blood and through which they give off their wastes.

Even when seated and listening to something we enjoy, we get fidgety and must move, shifting weight from one buttock to the other and making other adjustments. In standing, we shift weight from one leg to the other.

Any concept of good posture as freezing in some one particular position is inherently invalid. There is, of course, such a thing as poor posture. If, for example, one slouches in a round-shouldered position for prolonged periods, tissues on the convex side of the curve are stretched while those on the concave side tighten and are under strain. The strain may be enough to cause neck, shoulder, or low back pain.

Poor posture may be due to impaired muscular control, as in poliomyelitis or muscular dystrophy, or to weakness simply for lack of sufficient muscular activity. It may have psychological roots. Anyone confronted, for example, with an individual who slouches, with arms hanging slightly forward of knees and head drooping, and announces, "I have never felt better in my life," would know instantly that he is lying to others or to himself. Such a posture is associated with dejection and depression. On the other hand, a person who walks rapidly, arms swinging vigorously, head up, obviously is far from depressed.

The emotional state is reflected in posture and movement. There are those who say that if you wish to improve your emotional state, you should improve your posture. Possibly the converse obtains.

A good posture is one with which one is comfortable and which requires no inordinate amount of conscious effort. The back has normal curves and they should be maintained within certain limits. The spine is a column that must be supported and balanced to avoid toppling over. The muscles perform this function. Any extreme curve in the spine requires an inordinate amount of muscular work to maintain balance, and the excessive demand on the muscles may lead to fatigue and exhaustion at the end of the day and eventually may cause pain.

No one posture, as we have noted, can be maintained for more than a short period before it becomes uncomfortable. Small shifts are normal. But when posture generally—shifts and all—is well removed from the normal range, imposing undue stresses and strains, it is bad posture. Since posture is influenced by many factors—including the mental image a person has of himself as a human being and the position he takes about the world and his relationship with it, as well as what he views as normal posture and what he has become habituated to—it is not easy to change. But it can be changed.

Generally, in standing, the back of the head, apex of the thoracic spine, buttocks, and heels should all be in line; all of these areas, if one were standing back to a wall, should touch the wall. There should be a gap between wall and back of the neck, another between wall and area extending from buttocks to behind the chest; both of these are normally the areas of lordosis. This is good basic posture; it is not to be maintained constantly; minor shifts from it are entirely permissible.

In sitting, a good basic position is with soles of the feet flat on the floor, shank perpendicular to the floor, and hips flexed to 90 degrees. For those with back problems and even for others without such problems but who must sit for prolonged periods, support for the lumbar lordosis is important, which is why good secretarial and desk chairs are made with movable back segments that can be positioned for proper support.

Bed posture is important. The bed itself should be firm, almost as firm as the floor. This may sound uncomfortable, yet the fact is that most back-pain victims prefer, during a severe episode, to sleep on the floor since it is more comfortable for them than sleeping in bed.

The best type of bed is a rigid surface covered by a simple horsehair mattress. It is not easy to buy; salespeople are often reluctant to sell such a mattress because it is the cheapest type available; they much prefer to offer an expensive orthopedic mattress which, coupled with boards, springs and other intricacies, ends up approximating the effect of the simple, inexpensive horsehair mattress.

Lying flat, or almost flat, is the best position in bed. If one lies supine with the head supported by many pillows, the neck is flexed so that tissues in back of the neck are stretched while those in front are relaxed. Only a small pillow should be used. Since we do not remain in one position, prone or supine, all night, and roll from side to side, someone who uses no pillow will not be able to sleep comfortably on his side without a pillow to support the head. Without such support, there may be pain in the neck and upper back and shoulder. For proper support when lying on the side, a pillow should, when compressed by the weight of the head, be about equal in height to the distance between the tip of the shoulder and side of the face.

Generally, if one sleeps well and has no discomfort upon awakening in the morning, there is no need for concern about posture in bed. If there is pain on awakening, the possibility that it may be due to osteoarthritis, or wear-and-tear arthritis, may have to be considered. But not to be overlooked is a likelihood that a change of type of mattress or of type or height of pillow may help.

SHORT LEG

On occasion, back pain may be traceable to a difference in length of the legs. As we've noted, it is not unusual for the two sides of the body to be somewhat asymmetrical. Nor is it unusual for there to be a difference of as much as half an inch in the length of the two legs.

A good way to determine leg length is to measure from one point, the anterior superior iliac spine, to another, the medial malleolus. The anterior superior iliac spine is the bony bump on the hip, to the side of and slightly below the navel or belly button, the most prominent bone one can feel in that area. The medial malleolus is the most prominent portion of the bump on the inside of the ankle.

It is also possible to measure from the upper part of the hip bone, the iliac crest, although this is somewhat less accurate. If you use this method, make certain you measure, on each side, from a point midway between front and back of the upper part of the hip bone. Then measure, not to the medial malleolus on the inside of the ankle but rather, to the lateral malleolus, the outer protuberance of the ankle.

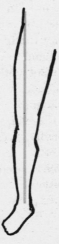

Significant leg-length discrepancy, greater than half an inch, it must be emphasized, is only occasionally a cause of back pain. When it is, a simple measure—use of a shoe lift—may be helpful. A shoemaker can provide this. It can take the form of an extra heel. Rarely is a sole lift necessary. A shoe lift also can be inserted within the shoe itself; this is usually more expensive but the extra expense may be justified in terms of appearance if experimental use of an external lift proves helpful.

TESTING FOR THE SHORT LEG EFFECT

Even when there is no fundamental anatomical difference in leg length, we have noted that a short leg effect productive of back pain can stem from a difference in how the legs are moved.

When we walk, we do so somewhat in the fashion of a revolving wheel, which happens to provide the best means of moving a weight from one spot to another on level ground. In the wheel, of course, the spokes, or radii, keep the rim a constant distance from the axle.

If you look at the body's hip joint as a kind of axle of a wheel, then the legs can be viewed as spokes.

The legs, of course, alternate in the process of transporting the body forward. This would be difficult if there were no joints at hips, knees, and ankles, for the feet then would scuff the floor or it would be necessary to bend to the opposite side every time a leg was moved forward. But with joints at hips, knees, and ankles, the leg can be momentarily shortened for easy walking.

If, however, any one of the joints on one side should be flexed excessively so that the leg is never fully straightened, then that leg will be shorter functionally, even though not anatomically, than the other.

This can have undesirable consequences, for with each step we take in walking, we must place the body's center of gravity over the leg that is bearing the weight at the moment so that we do not topple over. There is thus a constant oscillation as we walk, with the body's center of gravity moving about two inches to each side with each step. In effect, in walking we go through a process of losing balance and regaining it with one foot and then the other.

If a leg is shorter functionally, sideward motion is increased. As a result, greater than normal muscular activity is required, increasing the tendency to fatigue, and sometimes leading to pain in the back. And although there is always a limp, it sometimes may be so minimal that only a trained eye will notice it.

You can check for functional leg-length difference by looking at yourself when you walk and observing whether your body tilts more to one side than to the other. In addition, if you listen carefully, or have a friend do so, you can hear when you walk on a solid floor whether the impact of one foot is greater than that of the other.

A clue also may be provided by examination of a pair of shoes you have worn for a while to determine if wear on one heel is much greater than on the other. Some difference in wear may be noted on the sole but the heel is the best place to look because one strikes on a small area of the heel and any differences in wear are more easily observed.

Although it is rarely the sole cause of back pain, a functional leg-length difference may be a significant contributing factor. If you find such a difference, you may be able to compensate for it simply by using a heel lift. If this is not adequate, a sole lift as well may be tried.

If the functional leg difference stems from a relatively minor abnormal contracture of joints, it is sometimes possible to overcome it by getting into the habit of sleeping prone with no pillow. The weight of the buttocks and legs may help straighten hips and knees. The feet should be over the edge of the mattress, between the end of the mattress and the footboard;

otherwise the feet will rest on the toes and some flexion will be maintained.

For more severe contractures, physical therapy—with stretching exercises, neuromuscular facilitation techniques, or other measures—may be required. Such therapy can be obtained, by law, only through a medical prescription.

TENSION

Some people can tell readily enough when they are emotionally tense. For them, there are such obvious indications as gurgling in the stomach, cramping in the abdomen, diarrhea. But in many emotional tension is manifested only in the normal biological way: by increased muscle tension which, in less "civilized" times, served as preparation for fight or flight.

And many people with back pain stemming from muscle tension induced by emotional tension do not realize they are tense. Asked whether they consider themselves to be highstrung individuals, many respond with an emphatic negative. Yet examination reveals abnormally tensed muscles.

These people often must be taught how to determine for themselves—how to actually feel—the tension in their muscles. Once they are able to do this, they are often able to achieve relaxation of the muscles.

At ICD, we often ask such patients simply to try to let themselves go loose—to bend over at the waist and just let their arms hang loose, relaxed, "flopping" around. We ask them to raise shoulders to ears, hold them there briefly, then let them loose, and after that to try to push them down to the floor and then again let them relax. We ask them also to move shoulders forward and back, up and down, and in a circle, "loosening" them up through motion. And we ask them to notice the "feel" of a muscle when it is no longer tensed.

To get that feeling generally requires no prolonged effort. To deliberately relax muscles often enough during the day so that even though emotional tension may persist the muscles are not held in tension for prolonged periods is more difficult—but only in the sense that it is necessary to remind oneself to make the effort.

If a patient is tense enough to have pain, the pain usually will appear in the neck and upper back first—across the root of the neck and upper back, occasionally extending to the occipital protuberances, the bumps behind the ears.

If you experience such pain and place your hand on the root of the neck in the back, nearer the neck than the shoulder, you will feel that the muscles there are tense and tender. If you rub the area with your fingers, you are likely to feel some tenderness but also some sense of relief. While it is somewhat more difficult to do, you may be able with your hands to feel similar tension and tenderness in the low back as well.

DISK PROBLEMS

To determine conclusively for yourself whether you have a painful back as the result of an intervertebral disk problem is difficult if not impossible; for that, expert medical diagnosis is usually required. Yet you may be able to establish without great difficulty whether there is a *probability* of a herniated disk.

First, consider the symptoms. While back discomfort may be a symptom of a herniated disk, the most prominent complaint usually is pain down the leg and on the outer side of the foot, sometimes accompanied by numbness, "pins and needles" sensations, and weakness. There may also be some difficulty in standing on tiptoes.

With the aid of a friend or family member, you can go a step farther. While lying on your back, have the other person slowly raise your legs, one at a time, while you keep knees straight. Generally, he should be able to elevate each leg up to an angle of at least 80 degrees with the bed. If one leg can be raised to 80 or 90 degrees but the other can be raised only to 30 or 40 degrees without producing severe pain up the back, this may be an indication of a herniated intervertebral disk.

The leg-raising test cannot be relied upon absolutely—and, in fact, there is no test used in any area of medicine that is always positive in the presence of disease and always negative in its absence. There is uncertainty related to the limits of human knowledge and skill. For that reason, any conscientious physician always weighs the results of one test against the results of others and also takes into account the details of the patient's history.

And so, in any of your own evaluations, you must be prepared for some measure of uncertainty. In the leg-raising test, and in other tests as well, it would not be surprising, too, if you find yourself able to perform better one day than another. No person, afflicted or not, performs any function at precisely the same level from one day to the next or even at different times on the same day.

MUSCLE TESTS

Among the most important tests you can perform are those that may pinpoint the specific muscle weaknesses that may be causing backache.

Although we have previously discussed the significant role of muscles, it can be helpful to take up the subject again briefly here in connection with muscle testing.

In working, muscles contract; they always pull, never push. The system is such that usually one muscle opposes another; for example, one contracts to bend a leg and an opposing one contracts to straighten it. If each muscle of a pair is to contract smoothly, each must also relax smoothly. Failing this, muscle movement, because of the opposing forces, is "jerky," and such jerky, uncoordinated movement may cause injury.

Muscle activity is integrated by the central nervous system. Nerves sense the positions of various parts of the body and the tension in various muscles, tendons and ligaments, and relay the information to the spinal cord and brain, from which then stem messages to bring about coordinated relaxation and contraction. Since the excitatory state of these nerves is different at different times—before and after meals, with changes in barometer, weather, emotional state—coordination varies, and with such variations there are differences in one's capacity for work and exercise, for most effective and best-coordinated and safest use of muscles.

Beyond a likelihood that a muscle may be injured when movement is not well coordinated, there is a likelihood of injury when a weakened muscle is called upon to perform what otherwise would be a perfectly normal task.

Physical fitness is rare in the United States and in most so-called civilized countries. Especially in the United States, it is much talked about but not often achieved. Ours is an essentially sedentary existence. Few of us any longer have jobs requiring any great amount of sustained physical effort. We ride everywhere, even two and a half blocks to a supermarket. We ride elevators, even to go from one floor to the immediate next one. Few of us participate in sports on any regular basis—except possibly for the sports of turning on and off television sets and carrying food and drinks to our lips, which, while excellent exercises for wrist and fingers, do nothing for our backs.

Our sedentary way of life tends to weaken muscles, to impair coordination through disuse, and to encourage contractures. Our sedentary life is the primary cause of back pain. It is no accident that among all physicians those with most back pain are the psychoanalysts who sit in chairs much of the day.

Muscle pain occurs as a protest if at any time muscles are

called upon to do more than they are fit to do. When so over-burdened, they go into spasm; and this amounts to going "on strike" against what they view as excessive demands.

In the vast majority of the 5,000 patients with back pain we have seen at ICD—and the experience has been the same at other medical centers—the pain was the result simply of insufficient musculature.

The best test for evaluating muscular fitness was developed years ago by Dr. Hans Kraus, of the New York University School of Medicine's Department of Rehabilitation Medicine, in collaboration with Dr. Sonja Weber. It is a most valuable test and one you can use for self-evaluation, provided you understand the principle behind it.

It is a test of *minimal* muscle fitness, as Dr. Kraus has repeatedly emphasized, although even some professional users of it have forgotten this. What its developers found in extensive studies was that most people who have at least the level of muscular strength and flexibility needed to pass the test do not have back pain or have it infrequently. Those who do not meet the test standards do tend to have a high incidence of back pain.

But it is important to note that some who fail to meet the test criteria have never had back pain, and others who exceed the criteria do have back pain. There is no mystery about this; the reason is simple. Back pain stemming from muscular causes does so when demand exceeds capacity. If there is little demand, extremely weak muscles may produce no trouble, which accounts for the fact, for example, that a back-pain sufferer who goes to bed and stays there, making few movements, gets relief. On the other hand, if the demand is great, beyond the usual, the level of strength must be beyond the usual. A weight lifter, for example, can hardly do with muscles that may be adequate for a housewife.

The muscle strength–muscle pain relationship can be

likened to the relationship between the height of a dam and the water behind it. If the height of the dam is taken to represent the ability of muscles to perform while the amount of water represents the amount of work demanded of the muscles, and any overflow of water over the dam represents pain, then the overflow, or pain, will occur if there is only a moderate amount of water but the dam height is low, and it will occur even if the dam height, or muscle strength, is great but the quantity of water, or demand, is unusually greater. Even the best-trained athlete occasionally has pain when he makes a superhuman effort to exceed his usual standard.

Both in the course of his specialty training and for a time thereafter, the medical author worked with Dr. Kraus, who is very emphatic about the relationship between demand and ability to meet demand. Unfortunately, some of those who use Kraus' principles are not as fully aware of the importance of the relationship. Since my work with Dr. Kraus, I have used the Kraus-Weber test routinely. It is most valuable, but other testing is needed for patients who, although they meet the Kraus-Weber test requirements, still have pain which appears to be based on excessive demand.

In such cases, a study may be needed of the patient's job, going beyond job title and general description of his work, considering the specific activities he must engage in. Many people say, and believe, that they are very active when in fact they are not; and the reverse holds true. It is important to remember that in most jobs, work is not done at a constant rate; there are peaks and valleys during the day, and greater and lesser need for muscular exertion. If one watches construction workers, it is obvious that much of the time many of them are not called upon for great physical effort; only during relatively brief periods each day may they have to exert themselves to the maximum. The capacity of muscles for work must be great enough to meet maximum demand, not just average demand.

At ICD, because we see some patients, a small percentage of the total, who must do extremely heavy work, we have developed methods of mimicking such work, using extreme isometric exercises and pickup and carry tests in which the loads consist of sand made heavier by addition of water.

The Kraus-Weber test can be used to help determine whether inadequate muscle strength or flexibility may be a factor in your back pain. Later, it can be used as a measure of your progress in increasing strength and flexibility. Once you progress beyond the level called for by the test, you can still make use of it to measure further advances through variations and increased repetitions of the test exercises.

Thus, one part of the test, for example, calls for you to sit up, first, with knees straight and hands behind the back while your feet are held in place; then to sit up with knees and hips flexed. As you get stronger, you can go on to do sit-ups with knees both straight and flexed and with trunk in rotation; and, as you progress still further, sit-ups with feet unsupported and with knees straight and then with knees partially flexed.

In taking the test, get comfortable. Remove shoes, relax, proceed in unhurried fashion. The test exercises are not meant to evaluate speed. When done slowly, they are a bit more difficult and provide a better indication of muscle capabilities. In addition, any risk of hurting yourself is reduced.

In doing the exercises, keep your mouth open and inhale and exhale with your mouth open. Prior to any straining effort, consciously inhale through the mouth and let air out so the exhalation is readily audible to someone three or four feet away, and continue to inhale and exhale this way during the effort. With such breathing, you do not increase blood pressure and impose excessive strain on heart, lungs, or blood vessels.

Follow the instructions for each test—exactly.

1. Lie on your back on the floor, hands clasped behind the

neck. With knees straight and legs touching each other, lift your feet until they are ten inches above the floor. Now hold this position, feet in the air, for ten seconds if you can. If you can do

so, you pass the test and that means that your hip-flexing muscles have normal strength. If you fall short, record the actual number of seconds you can maintain the position, as a base line for future comparison.

2. Again, lie flat on your back on the floor, hands clasped behind the neck. Either have someone grasp your ankles to hold your feet down or place your feet under a bed, sofa, or other heavy furniture piece that can hold them. Now, with hands still clasped behind your neck and with elbows back, try to sit up by curling or rolling yourself up. This is a test of whether, working together, your abdominal muscles and your hip-flexing iliopsoas muscles have sufficient strength to handle your body weight. It is a relatively easy test. To pass it, only one sit-up is required.

3. Once more, lie flat on your back on the floor, hands clasped behind the neck. Now, however, your knees should be

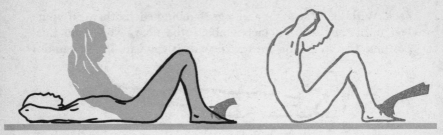

bent, and with ankles held down by someone else, or by a heavy piece of furniture, you are to try to curl up into a sitting position. In this test, with knees flexed so that your heels are as close as possible to your buttocks, you are eliminating the action of the hip-flexing muscles and determining almost entirely the strength of the abdominal muscles. Again, only one sit-up is required.

4. Now, to test the muscles of the upper back, turn over on your stomach and place a doubled-up pillow under your hips (not under your stomach). Have a friend or family member hold your ankles to the floor with one hand and steady the lower half of your body with the other hand placed over the buttocks. With hands clasped behind the neck, first raise your elbows off the floor and keep them off, next raise your chin, and then raise the trunk—so that elbows, chin, and trunk are all off the floor. Hold this position, if you can, for ten seconds.

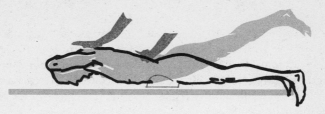

5. This is a test of lower back muscle strength. Your starting position is much the same as in test 4, prone, with pillow under hips. Now, however, have the friend or family member place one hand on the upper back and one on the lower back at about waist level. Your objective is to lift both your legs with knees straight, and to keep them elevated for ten seconds.

6. This is the final Kraus-Weber procedure and tests the flexibility of hamstring and back muscles and other structures. Stand erect in bare or stockinged feet, feet together, hands at the side. Let your head and arms droop forward and, keeping the knees straight, try to touch fingertips to the floor, without forcing or "bouncing" yourself down. If you cannot pass this test, it is not because of height; as relative size of arms and legs remains the same, tall people should have no more difficulty touching the floor than short people. Failure to pass is a result of shortening and tension of back muscles and hamstrings, the muscles in the back of the thighs.

Are these tests as valid for women as for men? Indeed they are.

A few years ago, the medical author was asked to speak at a YWCA about ski conditioning exercises. During the talk, I dwelled at some length on the importance of adequate muscle strength, endurance, and elasticity and in particular stressed the importance of abdominal muscle development and the value of sitting-up exercises for this.

Waiting politely during the talk, a young woman in the audience lost no time after it was over, immediately protesting, "But, doctor, women can't do a sit-up!" Fortunately, my wife was in the audience. I asked her to come up on stage, and being in excellent physical condition, she demonstrated that a well-conditioned woman could do sit-ups repeatedly, with knees flexed and knees straight, with ease.

The six Kraus-Weber tests are valuable for both men and women. They can indicate present strengths or weaknesses. They are tests for meeting *minimum,* not maximum, levels of muscular fitness.

If you failed any one, you have an immediate indication of a clear-cut weakness—and, quite likely, a clue to a cause of back pain.

If you passed all six, you have, we must keep emphasizing, at least minimal fitness. If, regularly or even just occasionally, you place more than minimal demands on the muscles at work, around the house or grounds, in some sport or other nonwork activity, minimal fitness may not be enough. Thus, passing the six tests may not eliminate muscle weakness as a cause of your back pain. You have to consider the demand factor.

At ICD, as we have indicated, and at other centers as well, about four of every five patients with pain in the back have that pain because of musculature inadequate to meet their needs. All told, the majority of the patients we have seen at ICD would have been able, if they had had available the information in this chapter, to diagnose their own problem and, by using the procedures to be detailed later, could have done much, and perhaps all that was needed, to overcome the problem and the pain.

CHAPTER 4

IF MEDICAL DIAGNOSIS

IS NEEDED

Under certain conditions, there is obvious need for expert medical attention.

If other symptoms, no matter how seemingly unrelated, are present along with back pain, medical diagnosis is called for because the backache may be related to those symptoms. As we have noted, back pain may stem from many nonback conditions, including peptic ulcer, prostate disease, kidney disease, retroverted uterus, fibroid tumors of the uterus, disturbances in the fallopian tubes. Any unusual stomach sensations, urinary disturbances, or menstrual problems that are coincident with back pain call for expert diagnosis.

If back pain is not relieved by conscientious application of the measures suggested later in this book, medical advice should be sought. For one thing, even if no other nonback symptoms are present, a subtle nonback condition may exist. Or the lack of relief may be due to failure, even a minor failure, to apply treatment measures properly.

If it should be necessary to seek medical help, choosing the right physician is, of course, a critical matter.

WHICH DOCTOR

It is generally best to start with one's family physician or an internist. He may be able to cope successfully with your problem himself. If not, he can guide you to a specialist best qualified to deal with it. It can be difficult for any patient to decide, on his own, which type of specialist to consult, and haphazard sampling may be expensive in both money and needlessly prolonged pain.

The family physician or internist may refer to a gynecologist the woman in whom he has grounds to suspect that back pain may be related to fibroid tumors, to a gastroenterologist the patient in whom he suspects some connection with a peptic ulcer.

Often, the family physician will refer a patient with a seemingly difficult back problem to a physiatrist, a specialist in physical medicine, if one is available in the community or nearby. Unfortunately, physiatrists are not in abundant supply. With less than a thousand in the whole country, some cities are without one and some states have only one or two. If available, a physiatrist is often the specialist of choice because of his prime interest in functioning of bones, nerves, and muscles.

An orthopedic surgeon, whose prime interest lies in bones and their integrity, is often of help. Other specialists may be needed in specific cases. For diseases of prostate, kidney, or urinary tract, a urologist may be required. An internist may be needed if the back pain is associated with disease of the heart or circulation. For example, a dissecting aneurysm of the aorta, a disease of the body's major trunk artery, can give rise to agonizing back pain, and its definitive diagnosis requires study by a cardiologist, an internist specializing in disorders of the heart and related structures.

Low back pain sometimes may be associated with blood vessel (vascular) disease of the legs. When it is, the pain may also appear in the buttocks and in the legs after a brief period of walking, may disappear with rest, and may occur again with further walking. Such a problem lies in the province of the specialist in vascular disease, either an internist with special knowledge and experience in vascular disease or, if surgery may be indicated for relief of the problem, a vascular surgeon.

A neurologist may be called for when nerve involvement is suspected, as the result of either pressure from a herniated intervertebral disk or from a tumor in the spinal canal, or even pressure elsewhere.

An endocrinologist, a specialist in glandular diseases, may be needed in cases in which back pain may be related to hormone imbalances. For example, the thyroid gland produces a hormone, thyroxin, and when levels of this hormone are not appropriate, one result may be back pain.

In a condition called osteoporosis, bones, including those in the spinal column, thin out, become weak, and may collapse as the result of loss of calcium from the bone framework. While osteoporosis, which tends to occur frequently in women after menopause, may cause major fractures with collapse of the vertebrae, more commonly it produces minor cracks in bone which may pull on the periosteum, the fibrous membrane surrounding bone, and in so doing may cause pain. The cracks sometimes are detectable on x-ray. Because calcium control— and, therefore, osteoporosis—may be related to hormone levels, an endocrinologist may be needed to help establish what the hormone levels are and what medication may be useful in correcting imbalances.

Where emotional problems seem to be contributing to back pain, psychiatric help may be valuable.

DIAGNOSTIC PROCEDURES: WHICH ARE NEEDED WHEN

Among the most important of all aids to medical diagnosis—for backache or any other problem—is the patient's history. Often it reveals valuable clues that can greatly narrow the search for causes, saving much time and effort.

For back pain, information about the nature of the pain itself can be significant, and it is often helpful if a patient uses a diary to keep tabs on the pain. Is it mild, moderate, or severe? What is its quality? Is it burning pain? Is it constant or intermittent? What time of day does it usually appear? Does it occur after any particular types of activities? Do certain activities make it disappear? Does coughing, sneezing, or straining during a bowel movement affect the pain for better or worse? Does eating make it better or worse? If eating does change the pain in any way, do certain foods seem to make the difference? Is the pain related to the menstrual cycle? Are there pins-and-needles sensations, or paresthesias, associated with the pain?

Let's consider briefly the possible significance of some of these aspects of back pain. The severity of the pain is not necessarily related to the seriousness of the cause. However, certain types of irritative pain—such as the pain accompanying fracture of the spine or fracture of a rib—are excruciating. Muscle spasm pain alone may be quite severe but rarely to the point of being intolerable. Trigger-point pain may range from mild to very severe. The early pain associated with a herniated intervertebral disk will be very severe, and is due in large part to the muscle spasm associated with the herniation, but usually the pain will tend to diminish fairly rapidly. A burning type of pain may indicate irritation of nerve fibers. Paresthesias, pins-and-needles sensations, may be due to interference with blood supply or irritation of nerve roots by a tumor, by a herniated disk, or by a muscle in spasm. Pain in the back late in the day may be due to emotional tension which frequently builds up during the day and, in the process, builds up muscle tension which may lead to back pain.

It is important for the physician taking a patient's case history to establish whether there is any record of diseases of muscles, bones, or joints in the patient or in the family. He may also obtain clues from any history of other disease—tuberculosis (which may affect bones), cancer, heart or blood vessel conditions, colitis, menstrual disturbances, and still others—in the patient or the family.

THE PHYSICAL EXAMINATION

This is the next most important diagnostic procedure. It will include measurements to determine whether the pelvis is level, examination of the spine for any abnormal curvature, and checks for muscle tension. The range of motion of joints will be tested.

A thorough physical examination may include measurement of chest and abdomen and a check to see whether breathing is predominantly through the chest cage or abdomen. People who use their abdominal muscles for breathing tend to have stronger abdominal muscles than do those who use chest muscles.

In examining the back, the physician will look for any trigger points, any nodules, any small herniations of fat. He will be looking as well for any other masses such as tumors, either benign or malignant, that may be present in the back.

Additionally, he will be checking for spina bifida which, occasionally, may produce back pain in otherwise apparently normal people. In spina bifida, bones in the back of the spinal column have failed to unite during intrauterine development, leaving an open space. While this opening may produce no symptoms in itself, muscle attachments are located somewhat off-center because of the opening, putting them at a mechanical disadvantage. Because of this, back muscle strength which may be adequate for an individual without spina bifida may not be for the patient who has the abnormality. Actually, almost 25 percent of "normal" people have spina bifida.

X-ray studies of the spine may be needed. An x-ray is, basically, a shadow rather than a picture. And just as any individual's overall shadow does not show what he looks like, so an x-ray may not indicate directly what is going on. But a physician can make valuable inferences from an x-ray shadow. For example, while intervertebral disks themselves cannot be seen on x-ray because they are radiolucent, bone is radiopaque and can be seen; and where the vertebrae are abnormally close together rather than showing normal spacing, the physician can infer that something must have happened to the disk between, and that something usually is degeneration or herniation.

One cause of pain low in the back which may also be referred to the hip and groin is hip joint disease. Severe arthritis of the hip joint may lead to painful nerve irritation. The range of motion of the hips therefore will be tested, and hip x-rays may be made.

Pain in the thigh that may radiate to buttock and low back may be due to bursitis in the hip joint area. This is usually readily diagnosed because the most severe pain is immediately over the most lateral bony ridge of the "hip joint." Actually, this is not the hip joint at all but a bulge on the femur bone called the greater trochanter. A bursa is a liquid-filled sac which performs a lubricating function, helping to avoid any fraying of muscles as they slide over rough bone. A bursitis here, as in a shoulder, for example, may be treated by cortisone injection or by oral administration of a drug such as phenylbutazone.

Other diagnostic tests may be required depending upon circumstances. If backache may be due to some form of arthritis, blood counts and other tests for rheumatoid arthritis, gout, and related diseases are needed. If a rare condition such as Paget's disease of bone or a benign or malignant bone tumor is suspected, suitable tests will be carried out. It should be emphasized that simply because a test for some specific disease is done is no indication at all that the patient actually has that disease. Much more often, tests are carried out to exclude any possibility that certain diseases may be present.

In some circumstances, special x-ray studies may be required. Tomography is a procedure in which the x-ray tube is made to rotate. With the rotation, all tissues in the body can be made to blur except for the tissue at the level at which the x-ray tube is focused. In effect, tomography can "slice" a bone for examination, providing a more precise indication of a bone tumor, fracture, or other abnormality.

On occasion, one or more of many other possible tests may be used. A spinal tap—in which a needle is introduced into the spinal canal and some of the spinal fluid is withdrawn for laboratory study—may be required if there is a suspicion that back pain may just possibly be related to a disease such as meningitis affecting the spinal cord. In addition to fluid withdrawal, pressure measurements can be made to determine whether spinal fluid flow may be obstructed, as would happen with a tumor of the spinal cord or surrounding structures. After such measurements and the fluid withdrawal, a radiopaque dye can be introduced to replace the withdrawn fluid. This is called myelography. The dye, which is usually an oily substance containing iodine, fills the lower part of the spinal canal; and when x-rays of the area are then taken, the column of iodized oil has a characteristic shape in most individuals. If the shape of the column is distorted, it may be because a tumor, benign or malignant, or a herniated intervertebral disk is producing the distortion.

Once, myelograms were done in many patients with back

problems even when surgery was not contemplated. Today, at most medical centers experienced in such problems, myelography is used only when the decision for surgery has been made and the procedure then can be helpful in indicating the level at which the operation should be carried out.

Today, for diagnostic purposes, a newer test, electromyography, has replaced myelography. Electromyography is similar to electrocardiography in that it picks up the body's own electrical potentials. During the test, the electrical potential generated by muscle fibers is amplified, and the signals can be recorded on tape or played through a loudspeaker. An experienced electromyographer can distinguish many abnormalities simply by listening to the sounds.

The test requires insertion of very fine, coated needles into various muscles in the back and in the legs or arms, depending upon whether the complaint is in the upper or lower back. Unlike injection needles, these are solid, carrying wires down their center, and they can pick up electrical potentials from very localized areas of muscle fibers.

The electromyogram can distinguish between an intrinsic disease of muscle such as muscular dystrophy and an inflammatory disease such as polymyositis or dermatomyositis, and can also detect diseases of the spinal cord. If a patient has a primary disease of muscle such as muscular dystrophy involved in his backache, then the electrical potential will be diminished because of destruction of some of the muscle fibers by the disease.

If a nerve supplying a muscle has been destroyed, the muscle becomes so irritable that electrical potentials are generated almost all the time even when the muscle is not being contracted, and these are recognizable. Electromyography often makes it possible to locate any irritative or destructive lesion. Various muscles in the back and in the arms or legs can be tested, and knowing which nerves innervate which muscles, the physician can suspect from any abnormalities of potential in specific muscles whether, for example, a herniated disk is pressing on a specific nerve root.

In certain cases, conduction velocity studies are done. By stimulating a nerve at one point and then picking up the electrical wave as it passes another point or as it produces a muscle contraction, the physician can determine the speed at which messages travel in the nerve. Pressure on nerve roots can disturb conduction, and primary nerve disease may alter the speed of conduction.

While myelography is commonly followed by headache and the procedure itself is painful for some patients, electromyography and conduction velocity studies have no adverse side effects.

On rare occasions, other tests may be needed. Biopsy, in which small sections of muscles are removed surgically and studied under the microscope, can reveal muscle disease, including the painful muscle disease that may be produced by trichinosis caused by pork parasites. Pain in the low back and buttocks in a few instances may be due to obstruction of either the aorta or another artery, the common iliac. This possibility can be investigated by x-rays taken after a radiopaque material is introduced into the bloodstream.

Nor does this even begin to exhaust the armamentarium of tests and diagnostic procedures the physician has available today to help pin down seemingly mysterious causes of back pain.

Many tests to investigate possible backache causes have been developed specifically for that purpose. In addition, because many less common backaches can stem from conditions that have nothing directly to do with the back itself, tests developed to diagnose these conditions—tests used in urology, gastroenterology, gynecology, neurology, cardiology and still other medical specialties—can be employed when needed.

The fact is that the overwhelming majority of back-pain

problems stem from simple causes; that in many cases such causes can be established by intelligent sufferers for themselves; that when the backache victim cannot determine the cause, the physician almost invariably can do so—and, even then, in most cases it will be a simple cause readily found by the expert.

But even when the cause is not simple, when it is a rare cause, it is possible now in most cases for the expert physician to establish it. Nor does he have to employ every test in the book. Guided by the patient's history and the clues that may offer, and by his findings on physical examination and the leads he picks up from them, he can narrow the possibilities considerably, and then use a relatively few appropriate tests.

It would be too much to say that every cause of backache can be eliminated once found. It is difficult to eradicate entirely trichinosis or other parasitic diseases of muscles, but their suppression can be achieved. Very often, however, curative treatment is possible, sometimes with medication, sometimes with surgery—as, for example, surgery to correct an abnormality of the aorta or another blood vessel, or to remove a benign or malignant tumor that is causing back trouble.

CHAPTER 5

WHAT VALUE HEAT, COLD, COUNTERIRRITANTS, OTHER HOME REMEDIES—AND PAIN-KILLERS, TRANQUILIZERS, AND MUSCLE RELAXANTS?

Recently a friend brought his wife in for treatment for an acute back pain episode. An intense woman, given to sudden, jerky, poorly coordinated movements when under pressure, she had undoubtedly suffered a sprain because of one such movement, and the sprain had led to muscle spasm which caused her pain. After treating her, we suggested that she use at home, among other measures, one of the popular counterirritants. Her husband expressed amazement that we would prescribe any such "nonscientific, useless measure."

But in its place a counterirritant is not useless. Nor, necessarily, are other home remedies. They may in fact be useful in providing a measure of relief until medical help can be obtained and in supplementing a physician's treatment; in some cases, they may even avoid need for medical aid.

Some home remedies are in use because centuries, even millennia, of experience have established their value. And while we will cover many newer methods of back-pain relief in this book, we will not neglect older ones, including home measures, of proven value.

HEAT

One useful measure for relieving muscle spasm, which is so often the cause of back pain, is the application of heat. Many animals have learned its value and sit in the sun or seek out warm pools of water to relieve muscle spasm and pain. So-called primitive peoples all over the world have been aware of heat's value. American Indians, for example, would provide safe conduct, in the midst of warfare, to members of an opposing tribe seeking help at a warm mineral spring.

Spa therapy, with emphasis on warm mineral spring baths, has been relatively little used in this country but has long been popular in the Soviet Union and much of Europe for several reasons. First, heat relaxes muscle spasm and, in so doing, relieves pain. Dissolved minerals in spa water are supposed to have special value, but such claims remain very much in dispute. Investigators have added various minerals to ordinary heated tap water and have found no enhancement of value. There have also been studies in which minerals actually obtained from spa water by evaporation have been shipped elsewhere in dry form to be dissolved in water and have given the water no special virtue. It is quite possible that therapy at a spa may have special value for other reasons. The patient is in a relaxing atmosphere, away from work and other stresses, and his muscles may have more opportunity to relax, including those in spasm. Also helpful in relieving any pain is the expectation of being helped, and that expectation is to be found in most people who visit spas.

The one clearly established value of spa therapy is its use of heat—and heat, in many forms, can be used effectively at home. Heat from the sun, from a heat lamp, from a hot water bottle, from a heating pad, from a heat-retaining gel or mud-type pack, or from a water-heated Turkish towel—any of these can be used. And expensive methods of applying heat are generally not much more valuable than simple, inexpensive ones.

For most people, wet heat is most effective. But for others, including one of the authors, dry heat works best. And it can be worthwhile to experiment to determine which is preferable for you.

Wet or dry, heat to relieve muscle spasm should be applied for 20 to 30 minutes. Shorter application may not produce a full response. On the other hand, nobody with muscle spasm should remain, deliberately, in any one position for a period longer than half an hour since this may lead to stiffness, and then the pain of movement may be severe enough to induce more muscle spasm and reestablish the cycle of spasm-pain-spasm. After no more than half an hour of heat application, get up and move around.

Heat should be applied, generally, at least twice a day. Four times a day would be even more preferable if practical. Intense heat is not required. It is gentle heating that is most beneficial. If a heating pad is used, it should be set for the lowest heat and should be wrapped in a Turkish towel to avoid burns. Weights should not be used to hold a heating pad down and, in fact, the pad should be placed *on*, not under, the body so it does not carry body weight.

If moist heat is to be applied, it is important to make certain that the heating pad is designed so there can be no short-circuiting when a wet towel is placed around it. Heating pads so designed are available and may carry an Underwriters' Laboratory seal indicating that they are immersible in water. If there is no such statement, do not use a pad for wet heat applications.

A hot tub bath is often an effective measure for helping to relieve spasm and pain. It is superior to a hot shower and if you happen to like showers for cleansing, switch to a tub bath for spasm relief. The bath should last for half an hour. At some point before the 30 minutes are up, the water will begin to feel cooler. The body will have cooled off a small area of water immediately next to it; if you swish the water around with your hand, or move your body, you can bring into play warmer water. A whirlpool bath may be used, but essentially such a bath agitates the water, moving it about, and so increases heat provided for the body, and much the same result is achieved when you swish the water with your hand or move your body. The sole other benefit of a whirlpool bath is that a gentle form of massage may be provided if the stream is directed at the back.

Other forms of heat may be recommended by a physician or may be provided by him or, on his prescription, by a physical therapist. A steam cabinet may be helpful. Most commonly used is the Moistaire-R, which allows parts of the body to be steamed. The heat provided is gentle, unlike that to be found in steam cabinets used for weight reduction (which really achieve only temporary weight loss through excessive perspiration).

A heat lamp may be recommended. The luminous, or infrared, type of heat lamp is obtainable in a pharmacy. Like a heating pad, it should be applied over a Turkish towel to avoid burns, and care should be taken not to fall asleep while using it.

Another type of heat lamp, the nonluminous infrared, is not used at home but may be employed by a physician or physical therapist. It applies superficial heat of a slightly different wavelength than the luminous type. There have been some claims that the effect on spasm is greater, but we have not found that to be the case.

Deep heat treatment sometimes may be employed by physician or therapist. Most commonly, a shortwave diathermy machine is used. It produces a rapidly alternating electrical field that induces motion of molecules in body tissues so that the heat is not confined to the body surface. The patient feels a sensation of warmth, which is useful as a guide to avoiding overheating of deep tissues.

Deep heat treatment is also provided by microwave diathermy. The heat is somewhat deeper than with shortwave diathermy. Because the deep heat is achieved without significant superficial heating, the safety factor is somewhat less than for shortwave diathermy. There is also evidence that the wavelength assigned by the Federal Communications Commission is not the best one for therapeutic purposes. The medical author is not convinced that microwave diathermy is a useful addition to the armamentarium in its present form but could well be if the wavelength were modified.

The deepest form of heat therapy is provided by ultrasound. The sound waves, though beyond human hearing, vibrate deep in the tissues, agitating the molecules there and causing them to release heat. Some physicians think there may be additional useful effects beyond heating to be obtained with ultrasound therapy, but the medical author does not believe this to be true.

Provided it is used skillfully, ultrasound therapy is safe. Because there is little or no heating on the skin surface and the heating effect of ultrasound is very rapid and focused at a point deep under the skin, the ultrasonic head must be moved constantly to avoid damage of deep tissues. It is for this reason that home use is not permitted.

All deep forms of heat—shortwave and microwave diathermy

and ultrasound—have potential dangers under certain circumstances. They should not be used when a patient has any metal within the body—as, for example, after hip nailing or use of metal sutures after surgery. The metal may become overheated. For the same reason, clothing should be removed for deep heat treatment so that any metal snap fasteners, buttons, brassiere adjustment devices, etc., are not overheated. Deep heat treatment is contraindicated if the possibility of tumor or other disease as the cause of pain has not been ruled out.

While there is some opinion that deep heat is superior to superficial heat for relieving muscle spasm, there is as yet no firm proof. Ultrasound, however, does seem to be as effective in some cases in relieving trigger points as trigger-point needling or massage.

While the major purpose of heat treatment—whatever the type and whether applied at home or in a physician's office—is relaxation of spasm, exactly how heat achieves such relaxation is still not clear. There is some speculation—and thus far only that—that it may involve a reflex mechanism in which heat stimulates nerves and, as a result, blood vessels become dilated so that more blood flows and metabolism of muscles, in turn, is increased.

Heat is valuable but not curative for spasm. In most cases, it is helpful preparation for effective use of other measures. Unfortunately, many patients are subjected to repeated heat treatments and nothing more when they need more, usually a curative exercise program. One of our associates, a consultant to the New York State Workmen's Compensation Board, has told us of the enormous number of cases he sees in which patients have been treated many times a week for months on end with heat alone, experiencing temporary relief after each treatment and quick pain recurrence thereafter for lack of an essential program of exercises.

Unhappily, this practice appears to be so common that a

public warning is needed. There are obvious financial benefits from providing a long series of ministrations that do no more than offer temporary relief. Actually, while only a few physicians engage in such practices for deliberate financial gain, some employ heat treatment alone for lack of understanding of the need for coupling it with other measures.

COLD

It may appear to be contradictory at first blush, since heat is effective, for cold to be, too. Heat expands blood vessels. Cold does just the opposite. Yet, after cold is applied for a period of time, a secondary phenomenon occurs: the constricted vessels become fatigued and then relax and become markedly dilated. In the end, then, the effect of cold is essentially the same as that of heat.

Most people prefer heat, finding it more comfortable. A cold application—in the form of ice or an ethyl chloride spray—can be shocking. It may have some appeal in summer but certainly not in cold weather.

Yet, actually, cold is uncomfortable only for the first few minutes, after which the area to which it is applied becomes numb. With further cooling, a fleeting burning pain appears. But as the cooling continues, the burning pain quickly disappears (often in a matter of seconds) and the area becomes anesthetized. Once this anesthetized state is arrived at, cold should be applied further only for about five more seconds and then should be discontinued.

Properly applied, an ethyl chloride spray can be beneficial. While other spray chemicals are available for cooling, ethyl chloride is useful because it does not evaporate as readily and its cooling effect is somewhat deeper.

In applying ethyl chloride, the can should be inverted so the nozzle is down. The spray stream should be kept moving. Once a white, frozen patch appears on the skin, spraying should be stopped and the area should be wiped gently with the hand in order to warm the skin enough with hand warmth to prevent tissue damage. On occasion, a white discoloration of the skin may appear before freezing is achieved. At least for the first few times an ethyl chloride spray is used, it may be necessary to make certain that freezing rather than mere discoloration has been achieved. For this, a pin can be used. A merely discolored area will be sensitive to a pin prick; a frozen area will not be.

It should be remembered that ethyl chloride is flammable; no flame, therefore, should be brought anywhere near the spray.

Another precaution is important. The gas that develops as ethyl chloride evaporates is an anesthetic and, in fact, years ago was used for anesthesia. The gas is heavier than air; if it should concentrate around the patient, it may well put the patient to sleep. In fact, this once happened to the wife of one of the authors when he was spraying the back of her neck. She was on a couch, her head turned toward a corner at the back of the couch where the heavier-than-air gas could accumulate. She fell asleep, totally anesthetized. While harm does not invariably result, there are some people—those with heart problems, for example—for whom such an accident may be dangerous.

Preferably, during application of ethyl chloride, the patient should be seated or the face should be turned in such a way that any gas that evaporates can flow downward away from the nose. The room should be well ventilated, too. (Because other vapocoolant sprays are not flammable and may not cause general anesthesia, some physicians prefer them for home use despite their lesser effectiveness.)

When ethyl chloride is not available, ice may be used. Ice cubes or pieces of crushed ice placed in an ordinary pillow case and gently rubbed over the skin are often effective in relieving spasm. With ice, as with other hot or cold applications used to relieve spasm, the area covered should be much larger than the immediate site of pain. The ice should be rubbed gently, back and forth, and the water should be allowed to roll off the skin. No attempt should be made to dry the skin, since the water retains the cold and acts as an effective adjunct to the ice.

As with ethyl chloride spray, ice first has a shocking effect because of the temperature, followed by accommodation to the cold, then some burning pain for a few seconds, and finally anesthesia. Ice should be rubbed on for about 30 seconds more once anesthesia appears and pain is gone.

Pain sometimes seems to move after muscle spasm is relieved whether by spray, ice massage, or heat. It does not really move, however; as we've noted previously, it is pain awareness that shifts—now to any areas of pain that were present before but, being less severe, were not heeded in the presence of the more severe pain. We have all had the experience of suffering some injury, minor or severe, and being totally unaware of any pain at the time of injury because our attention was focused on something else of greater importance at the moment; later, the pain became apparent enough. Similarly, we pay attention to a most painful area and may ignore other areas of lesser pain.

When, after application of heat or cold to relieve pain in one area, another area is found to be painful, that area can be treated as the first one was.

Properly applied, neither heat nor cold is damaging, and either may be used three or four times daily when required.

Always, after the use of heat or cold or any other measure for relief of spasm, gentle movements should be used to mobilize and stretch the previously spasmodic muscles.

COUNTERIRRITANTS

Whatever their form—old-fashioned mustard plaster or any of the more modern creams or liquids containing oil of wintergreen or methyl salicylate—counterirritants are useful.

They may work in two ways. The irritation they produce may be enough to provide some distraction so there is less awareness of the original pain. But, in addition, the irritation causes a nervous reflex response that leads to dilatation of blood vessels, and, in that, counterirritants have an effect similar to application of heat and cold.

In terms of effectiveness, there is little difference among most counterirritants, but there are, of course, differences in odor, greasiness, and convenience of use which may make one preferable to another.

Counterirritants generally have more of an effect when used after heat applications, since the heat opens the skin pores and allows greater absorption of the counterirritant preparation. Some people find this beneficial; others dislike the added irritation.

If you find the relief you obtain from heat or cold inadequate, it may turn out that a counterirritant, used either alone or as a follow-up to heat application, may help.

There is no danger in the use of counterirritants for most patients with back pain. But if back pain is associated with leg pain and spasm of leg muscles, anyone with vascular (blood vessel) disease or diabetes should beware of using a counterirritant, or even heat, on the legs, although either or both may be applied safely to the back. With vascular disease or diabetes, the leg arteries may be affected, and while one major effect of heat or a counterirritant is dilatation of blood vessels, another is an increase in local metabolism. If, because of disease, a vessel cannot dilate, it is unable to supply the additional circulation and nourishment required for the increased metabolism, and tissue starvation may result.

It must be emphasized that the use of any or all of the measures already discussed for relieving spasm accomplishes only that. None of them increases muscle strength, endurance, or coordination. That is equally true of massage, another valuable spasm-relieving measure to be discussed in Chapter 7. But the relief of muscle spasm is vital not only for amelioration of pain but also to allow going on with measures to improve muscle condition so as to help prevent recurrences.

BED REST

For a very severe backache, bed rest can be an effective measure. As we've seen, the spasm involved is a kind of biological splint; the muscles have gone into involuntary contraction as a way of reducing the motion of an injured area. The greater the threat of motion, the more the spasm and resulting pain. In bed, the threat of motion is considerably reduced and the muscles may relax.

But there are limits to how long bed rest may be used. Muscles become deconditioned and weak with remarkable rapidity. A patient placed at bed rest loses almost one third of the strength in the muscles of his thighs, for example, within ten days even if he has normal strength to begin with. Because of the rapid deconditioning, the period of bed rest should be limited to what is absolutely required. For most cases of severe back pain, no more than two or three days should be needed.

Many people make the mistake of trying only one home remedy at a time. Frequently combinations—such as going to bed for a few days plus heat, massage, and counterirritants—provide far better results. And various medications may also contribute substantially in themselves and when used with the other measures.

ANALGESICS

Analgesics, or pain-killers, which are commonly used to relieve various types of pain in various parts of the body, may be helpful for back pain. Aspirin is often useful and should be tried first.

There is still much mystery about how most drugs work. And aspirin is one of those whose mechanism of action is still not clear, although recent research suggests that it may counter the effects of a prostaglandin, one of a newly discovered class of body compounds which may be involved in producing inflammation and pain.

Aspirin is effective in many conditions because it has an anti-inflammatory as well as analgesic effect. It is often used in rheumatoid arthritis, including cases of rheumatoid arthritis in which the joints of the spine are affected, and its use is often beneficial. When inflammation is present in back conditions, as it may be after injury or in backaches associated with some diseases such as polymyositis and periarteritis nodosa, aspirin may have dramatic value.

Many people do well taking aspirin in its simplest, least expensive form. Patients whose back pain is particularly severe first thing in the morning may find that use of long-acting aspirin is helpful. Two tablets of such aspirin taken at bedtime may have an effect lasting long enough to reduce or eliminate stiffness and pain on arising.

If aspirin is not adequate, other medications, such as Darvon and Talwin, may be prescribed by a physician. These are nonnarcotics; in some cases, they are more effective, in some less so, than aspirin. They may have side effects for some people, but no drug, including aspirin, is entirely free of them. If any medication produces undesirable effects, a physician should be consulted immediately. Even if the undesirable effects are not life-threatening, they need not be suffered since there is usually another agent that may be used instead.

Occasionally, Demerol or morphine may be prescribed. While these drugs can be addicting when used over a prolonged period, their short-term use may be of great value. Unfortunately, we have seen patients with such an unjustified, overpowering fear of narcotics that they have refused a single dose and have gone through weeks of pain because the relaxation of the vicious cycle of pain-spasm-pain-spasm was not broken earlier as it might have been through use of Demerol or morphine.

TRANQUILIZERS AND MUSCLE RELAXANTS

The fact is that almost all tranquilizers have some degree of muscle-relaxing action and virtually all muscle relaxants have some tranquilizing effect. Agents considered to be primarily muscle relaxants seem to act more directly on muscles while providing some relaxation of emotional tension; those classified as tranquilizers relax emotional tension, and the relaxation of emotional tension helps to relax muscle tension.

A physician's choice of muscle relaxant or tranquilizer for a backache patient often depends upon how emotionally tense the patient is. One or the other may make a useful contribution to treatment for the immediate back episode.

DON'T HESITATE TO USE HOME REMEDIES

The value of home remedies can be great. Even if medical care is eventually required, the pain of an acute backache may be so agonizing that some measure of relief is needed prior to the arrival of a physician. Pain, as we have seen, can lead to spasm, and spasm can lead to pain. One feeds on the other in a vicious cycle, and the earlier the cycle can be interrupted, the better the chance for quickly aborting the painful episode.

There should be no hesitation in using home measures. The only danger is to rely on them entirely for relief of pain without getting to the cause of the pain.

CHAPTER **6**

ACUPUNCTURE AND

TRIGGER POINTS

She is a 41-year-old social worker, a woman respected for her professional abilities and also for her indomitable courage. She has managed to make her life a useful one despite the great handicap of congenital cerebral palsy. She has carried on despite repeated episodes of extreme severe back pain. Because of the abnormal way in which she must walk, her muscles are abnormally burdened and frequently rebel by going into spasm, producing the agonizing backaches.

For more than ten years, we have been seeing her at ICD, employing many methods of treatment which have helped reduce the frequency of the backache episodes at least to some extent. We have used many techniques to get her out of acute episodes, usually with success.

But recently she had an episode that resisted every measure we had previously used. Almost in desperation, we then tried applying concentrated pressure over certain acupuncture points. The relaxation of muscle spasm and relief of pain were gratifying. We noted, too, that her walking and balance improved dramatically; apparently the greater than usual relief achieved with the acupuncture point pressure also led to some diminution of the spasticity that accompanied her palsy.

Acupuncture, of course, has aroused considerable interest since American scientists have been able to go into mainland China and have found acupuncture very much alive and flourishing there. The ancient medical art of inserting needles into strategic points of the body to relieve pain has captured the imagination of the American public and excited considerable research interest among physicians.

Even for some years before this, we had been intrigued at ICD at finding a relationship, still not clear (as much about acupuncture still is not), between the needling of acupuncture sites and the needling of trigger points. And it appears that there is promise of backache relief in a nonneedling technique we have begun to use on certain acupuncture sites. It is a technique that can be put to use at home.

We have mentioned trigger points passingly before. We should consider them here again, in more detail, because of both their importance in themselves and the relationship they seem to have with acupuncture.

THE TRIGGER-POINT PHENOMENON

The importance of trigger points—also called trigger areas and trigger spots—in causing pain was discovered only shortly prior to World War II, and ever since they have commanded increasing medical attention.

The term "trigger" is apt because stimulation of these unduly sensitive little muscle areas—like the pulling of the trigger of a gun—can produce effects at another place, a target area. Apparently, impulses arising in a trigger point may bombard the central nervous system to produce referred pain.

The referred pain sometimes may be only dull and aching, but it also can be severe, sometimes even incapacitating. If the target area, the site of the referred pain, is pressed, there may be only a slight increase in discomfort. But if the same amount of pressure is applied to the trigger point, the pain increase in the target area is sharp.

Considerable mystery still surrounds the trigger-point phenomenon. How does a trigger point arise? At some time, virtually all of us experience the cramping of a calf muscle in a leg; millions of muscle fibers suddenly have contracted to knot the muscle. There is a theory that a trigger point may develop when, for some reason, perhaps under the stress of severe spasm, just a few thousand fibers tighten and form a localized knot which may persist even after the spasm disappears.

Whatever the mechanism of formation, when a trigger point is present and causing pain, treatment of the trigger point often brings dramatic relief. Within minutes, pain present for months may disappear completely, and sometimes permanently. Even when the relief is only temporary, it allows initiation of corrective treatment for a backache patient that otherwise could not be used.

The results of trigger-point treatment sometimes astonish even physicians who do not happen to be familiar with the phenomenon. We have a patient who has advanced, widely spread cancer of the spine and now is paralyzed below the waist. She developed agonizing pain between her shoulder blades. Although the attending physician and a consultant neurologist felt that the shoulder pain was due to the spread of the cancer, we were called for consultation and, on examination, found trigger points at the base of each scapula, or shoulder blade.

We suggested that the shoulder pain problem might be this:

The patient wanted to sit up. When she attempted to sit, however, she could not support her trunk over her pelvis because the muscles were paralyzed. In an attempt to compensate, she used other muscles which she had never used for the purpose, and strained them. Trigger points then developed and it was the trigger points, we suggested, which might be causing the pain.

We also suggested treatment for the trigger points, and two days later the attending physician called and asked us to provide the treatment. When we got there, we found on the patient's chart a note from the neurologist implying that the pain had to be due to the cancer and that trigger-point injections would be useless. But almost as soon as we injected the trigger points, the patient had relief of pain, and the relief persisted.

A week later we were called back because of other pain. Once the agonizing pain between the shoulder blades had been ended, the patient had become aware of pain elsewhere. She had also, in her efforts to sit up, been straining the trapezius muscle, which inserts on the base of the skull and goes across the upper back and neck. Injection of trigger points we found at the base of the skull gave her prompt relief.

Obviously, the trigger-point injections had no effect at all on the malignancy. Somehow, the injections had broken up the trigger areas and ended their pain-producing activity. But how?

The mechanism is still unknown.

Commonly, injections for trigger points include a local anesthetic. But the effect of a local anesthetic lasts only about an hour—as long as the effect of a dentist's injection of a local anesthetic into the gums lasts. If relief were due only to deadening of the trigger point, the relief should disappear quickly. Since it lasts for extended periods and sometimes may be permanent, some other mechanism must be involved.

Commonly, too, injections for trigger points include cortisone or a similar agent. Yet, we have given many injections containing only a saline solution and obtained exactly the same results as with injections containing both anesthetic and cortisone.

Moreover, we have been finding that simple needling of a trigger point, without injecting anything at all, is often just as effective as an actual injection. And there was a suggestion in that fact—in the effectiveness of just needling alone—of some possible connection with acupuncture.

There was another suggestion of the same thing in the fact that in many instances trigger-point sites coincide with acupuncture sites.

THE ACUPUNCTURE THEORY

Acupuncture (from the Latin *acus,* "needle," and *pungere,* "to sting") has been used in China for 3,000 years. According to legend, it had its beginnings in the experience of an ancient soldier who was struck by an arrow during a battle and noticed that he felt a sensation of numbness far removed from the actual site of the wound.

Acupuncture in China developed in conjunction with moxibustion, the burning of an herb at or near certain sites on the body. And Chinese traditional medicine has at its core a combination of acupuncture, moxibustion, use of herbs, breathing exercises, and therapeutic massage.

Acupuncture takes on added mystery for Westerners because there is no scientific explanation for how it may work. So far as many Western scientists are concerned, most traditional explanations are based on Eastern philosophy and are imaginary in whole or in part.

According to the traditional Chinese explanation, energy (called chi) circulates all through the universe under the control of forces called yin and yang, which correspond to the ebb and flow of any pair of opposing forces, such as light and dark, male and female, good and bad.

In the body six organs, the so-called solid organs (including liver, kidneys, and lungs) are under the forces of yin, while six hollow organs (including gallbladder, small intestine, and stomach) are under the forces of yang.

In the human body, energy, or chi, flows along twelve parallel lines, or meridians, which run the length of the body and its extremities. Most meridian lines are associated with major body organs, and chi flows along the meridian lines and through the organs in accordance with natural life rhythms. Those rhythms regulate functions that go on from day to day (for example, waste elimination), monthly (the female reproductive cycle), or seasonally (moods). According to the theory, a person is sick when the natural rhythm of the energy flow is disrupted or changed in some way. And acupuncture serves to restore the natural rhythm.

Along the network of meridians are more than 500 specific points. A needle inserted into any one of these acupuncture points along a meridian associated with a major organ is supposed to affect the functioning of that organ.

Traditionally, there are nine kinds of needles of varying lengths and sizes. Some are inserted less than half an inch; others go in several inches; some are left in place for only a few minutes; others remain in place for days. For some illnesses, repetitive treatments are required.

Based on complex laws believed to govern the relationship among various organs, an acupuncturist may insert his needles in sites along several meridians to treat a disorder in one organ. For stomach ulcers, for example, a point known as "stomach 43," situated above the division of the second and third toe, and another known as "liver 1," also in the foot, may be needled.

Why should needles inserted in two places in the foot affect stomach ulcers? Nobody knows. Some experiments indicate that electroresistance decreases all along a particular meridian line when acupuncture is applied.

An acupuncturist determines where to place his needles by taking the patient's pulse. In acupuncture there are twelve pulses, six in each wrist, corresponding to the twelve meridians. By feeling the rate and pressure of each, the acupuncturist is supposed to be able to establish which organ is ailing and causing the symptoms about which a patient complains.

Because of the widespread interest in acupuncture, it may be in order to range briefly just a bit afield here, beyond backaches, to consider the uses to which acupuncture has been put by some Western practitioners.

Dr. Felix Mann is a London physician who has practiced acupuncture for more than a dozen years. He is the author of several books on the subject and, in addition to being in private practice, offers a course for British physicians in acupuncture. Recently, at the State University of New York Downstate Medical Center in Brooklyn, Dr. Mann related his experiences.

"In acupuncture," he reported, "an illness is considered a weakness of some part of the body. For instance, in treating hay fever, I generally treat the lungs because they are part of the respiratory system. If it's the allergic type, then I might treat the spleen. It depends on which pulse is weak. If the lung is weak, then you treat hay fever one way; if the spleen is weak, you treat it another way. It doesn't make any difference whether one is allergic to cat hairs or dust."

In his experience, it takes an average of seven treatments to cure someone who has had hay fever for ten years, provided he responds at all to acupuncture. At first, the patient receives treatment about twice a week, then once weekly, then once every two weeks. Depending on individual circumstances, a patient might be cured permanently or might have to return once each season for booster treatment.

"Acupuncture," reported Dr. Mann, "can be used to treat any

ailment that is physiologically reversible. For example, a kidney stone is not physiologically reversible once it is there. But you can treat the kidney to reduce the chance of recurrence.

"The success rate of acupuncture depends on what I am treating. In some areas I may cure only 5 percent of the patients. I generally have a 75 percent success rate with migraines. With ulcers, I help two out of three. I can't cure angina pectoris [the chest pain associated with coronary heart disease], but I can get an improvement in perhaps half of the cases. If the patient can hardly walk before treatment, then he should be able to hike a couple of miles afterward."

Mann believes that acupuncturists should have conventional medical degrees because extensive knowledge of the body and basic medicine is helpful in using acupuncture. He estimates that there are 15 physician-acupuncturists in England, 300 in South America, about 1,000 in western Europe, and another 1,000 in Russia. However, he also estimates that there are about twenty times as many practicing acupuncturists who are not physicians.

How does he explain the mechanism of acupuncture? Mann says that he "wouldn't care one bit" if the reason for the effectiveness proved to be psychological, so long as it works. But he believes that acupuncture does work via the nervous system and that cures are a matter of stimulating the proper nerves.

"You can leave out the yin and the yang," he observes, "and just explain it in terms of ordinary medicine—not completely, but enough to show that it works by nerve reflexes. I am writing a book now which will explain acupuncture in neurophysiological terminology which I think will appeal more to physicians."

Both American and Japanese investigators have recently pointed out that according to modern medical concepts, many of the meridian points correspond to areas where nerves appear to surface from a muscle or where vessels and nerves are located relatively superficially, such as in areas between muscle and bone or between bone and joint. In addition, some of these points are considered "electropermeable points"; they are electrically less resistant than other areas.

One explanation of how acupuncture works to relieve pain is based on a "gate control" theory originally proposed by British and Canadian physicians who were concerned with pain mechanisms rather than with acupuncture. According to the gate control theory, stimulation of certain large fibers in sensory nerves—stimulation that might be produced by acupuncture needles—closes a kind of gate in the spinal cord. This could block pain impulses moving along a different set of smaller nerve fibers, preventing the impulses from traveling up the cord to the brain.

But while this might conceivably block pain impulses traveling along nerves to and from the spinal cord at areas from the neck down, it does not explain how acupuncture needles inserted in the arm, for example, can make possible dental extractions without pain. Recently, it has been proposed that there may be a second gate in an area of the brain, the thalamus, which closes to keep pain sensations from getting to the pain-sensitive area of the brain from below or above the spinal cord.

How acupuncture works to help internal diseases such as high blood pressure or asthma remains mysterious. Some investigators believe that stimulation of nerves on the skin may affect internal organs through reflex pathways. More than twenty years ago, Dr. Janet Travell, who was physician to the late President John F. Kennedy, determined that when certain trigger points on the chest are injected with procaine, prolonged relief from the chest pains of angina pectoris sometimes could be achieved. There have been experiments, too, in which scratching the skins of animals has led to changes in intestinal functioning.

MODIFIED ACUPUNCTURE FOR BACK PAIN

For some time at ICD, we have been finding that a modified acupuncture technique is often helpful for patients with back pain. As we have already noted, just plain dry needling of trigger points—without injecting anything at all—is often effective, fully as effective as injections. In acupuncture, a needle is inserted and rolled around.

Actually, one of the very early methods of treating trigger points involved using just a knuckle to press down and "break up" the points. At ICD, therapists do not use their knuckles but do use something only slightly different—a round, blunt object such as the hard cylindrical outer wrapper in which some cigars are packaged. They apply the cylinders, using them to exert pressure, not only over trigger points but also over acupuncture points. Unlike the trigger points, acupuncture points do not appear to be markedly tender. Yet pressure on them has proved to be helpful.

In evaluating any therapeutic measure, one must, ideally, go beyond whether the measure works or does not work. One should also try to explain how it works—to propose a theory that may provide the explanation, a theory that encompasses all the known facts, and seems reasonable. Beyond that, a final step is to determine whether the theory is sound and holds up.

We do not know how acupuncture works—what needles really do or what pressure over acupuncture points may do. We do know, however, that the pressure often works. We are continuing research to try to determine the mechanism and also to try to achieve greater benefits with the technique.

If you, in home checks, determine that you have trigger points which seem to be involved in your back pain, they may require injection or needling by a physician skilled in the technique. But it is quite possible that you may be able to treat them yourself without injection or needling.

In some cases, trigger points respond to ethyl chloride spray. You can use the spray (see Chapter 5) to "freeze" a trigger point. If necessary, you can repeat the spraying at intervals.

Alternatively, trigger points may respond to pressure applied with a hard cylindrical object. Those that we have thus far found most responsive to pressure are indicated on the accompanying illustrations.

You may also use pressure, with possibly good results, on certain acupuncture sites. The chart indicates those acupunc-

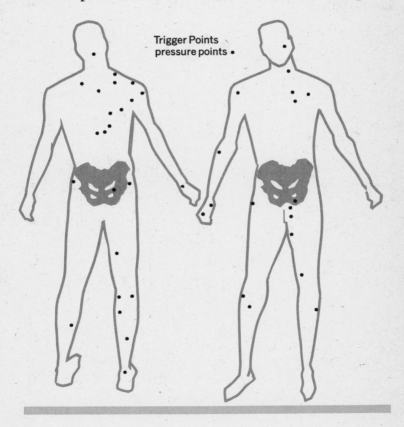

Trigger Points
pressure points •

ture points that have been found in studies at ICD to be most likely to be involved in back pain. Acupuncture points related to internal diseases are deliberately omitted from the chart. Their stimulation by a novice is to be avoided. Please confine your stimulation efforts to the points shown on the chart and do not experiment with other sites.

You will need to have a friend or family member apply the pressure. While there can be danger of infection from unsterilized acupuncture needles, there is no such danger when pressure is applied.

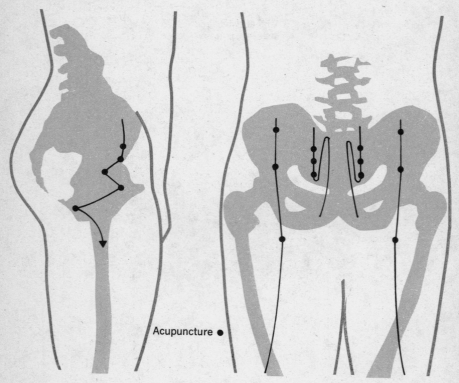

Acupuncture ●

It is easy enough to recall one particularly dramatic case indicative of how valuable pressure sometimes can be. The patient was a 56-year-old woman with very severe low back pain and with a trigger point that needed treatment, but she was extremely frightened of trigger-point needling. The trigger point was near an acupuncture point which we had found associated with low back pain, and we finally prevailed upon her to allow us to apply pressure with a cylinder to the acupuncture point. The pressure was applied for ten seconds and she screamed with pain. But then a smile crossed her face. "It doesn't hurt any more. My back feels fine," she exulted and promptly got down off the table and began to hop around in joy. We proceeded to calm her down and, now that the pain relief made it possible, got her started on the corrective exercise program she needed.

CHAPTER 7

MORE THAN ONE KIND

OF MASSAGE

One of the oldest of therapies, massage is often valuable for back pain. There are many forms, some of which can be used effectively at home. Licensed physical therapists use massage, including special types, along with other therapeutic techniques under medical direction.

A massage industry has been sprouting rapidly. In Los Angeles alone there are more than 150 massage parlors doing a $50 million a year business; and according to some estimates, Americans currently may be spending several hundred million dollars annually in commercial massage establishments, some of them good and some of them functioning as disguised bawdy houses.

Misconceptions about massage abound. There are people who believe that somehow massage can cure arthritis and sciatica, take off weight and even remove wrinkles, renew the heart, expand lung capacity, and strengthen muscles. It can do none of these—nor can it cure backaches, though it can help in specific ways.

We have seen many patients with agonizing back pain respond so well to massage that they no longer needed narcotics. The medical author recalls an experience with a very good friend who, in the midst of an attack so severe that she could not get out of bed, phoned and begged that a prescription for a narcotic be called to her druggist. Instead, I got to her as soon as possible and listened to her report that she had not slept for two nights and now could hardly even roll from one side of the bed to the other. Examination revealed severe muscle spasm, and the first measure I used was massage. Within just a few minutes, she was able to get out of bed and get to the bathroom.

HOW MASSAGE WORKS

One of massage's values is psychological, and although not easy to measure objectively, it could be of significance. Stroking of the body has a soothing effect. Children often respond dramatically to it, as every mother knows, and adults appreciate it even if they do not make their response so obvious. Dogs, of course, seek it out. And many other animals are sensitive to it, huddling together and licking and stroking each other.

There are physiological values as well. Whenever muscles contract, energy is consumed; chemicals obtained from food are oxidized and the process provides the energy required for muscle contraction. But the process leaves some residue, chiefly lactic acid. For continued activity, not only must more chemical fuel and oxygen be supplied; waste products also must be removed, and these are jobs for respiratory and circulatory systems.

The muscles themselves help get the jobs done, for as they contract and relax and to some extent rub against each other, they stimulate nerve endings and inform the nervous system of their activity. The nervous system then arranges for a stronger, faster heartbeat and a relaxation of blood vessel walls so more blood can circulate to bring nourishment and carry away wastes. At the same time, the breathing rate is increased so more oxygen is taken in.

Muscle activity helps in another way as well. Blood moving out from the heart through the arteries has pressure behind it to propel it forward. But there is no such pressure for return flow through the veins to the heart. Valves in the veins serve to keep blood from flowing the wrong way. But the return of venous blood, especially from the lower trunk and legs, depends upon contraction of muscles to "squeeze" it along.

Faintness and even outright fainting can occur in anyone standing still for an extended period. That's because, without muscle movement, blood tends to pool in the leg veins, not enough returns to the heart, and the heart then cannot pump enough to the brain.

But short of that extreme situation, with modern sedentary living muscular activity may be less than needed to prevent fatigue and dragged-out feelings. The fatigue of inactivity—of inadequate circulation and exchange of nutrients and waste products in the tissues—is as real as fatigue from excessive labor.

With emotional tension, too, there is muscle tension, and the state of muscular contraction increases energy needs yet interferes with the processes that can satisfy the needs.

Exercise can do much to overcome tired, dragged-out feelings by stimulating the circulatory and respiratory systems. But it can be difficult for a fatigued person to face the prospect of active exercise.

Massage, in effect, is passive exercise. It provides stimulation which can produce a response of the nervous system and in turn a response of the respiratory and circulatory systems. Massage also helps to relax muscles in spasm and thus to minimize the accompanying pain.

HOME MASSAGE

A simple, light stroking massage can be used at home to help relieve spasm. A comfortably warm room should be chosen and the patient should lie prone, undressed, with a doubled-up pillow under the hips, and with arms resting at the sides.

While alcohol rubs are often used in the hospital to help relieve irritation for patients in bed for prolonged periods, alcohol is not the best material for massage. A good material for home use is unscented talcum powder; one of the commonly used baby powders is fine. Dusted on the back, it allows the rubbing hand to slide easily over the skin, avoiding undesirable friction. Alternatively, a light mineral oil or even a cooking oil can serve as the lubricant. A small amount of oil should be placed on the palm, allowed to warm, and then applied to the patient's back and spread gently.

Whether the pain is in upper or lower back, light massage should start at the buttocks. Use the heels of the hands—the base of the thumb and the palm surface near the wrist. Press gently up on each side of the spinal column, avoiding pressure over any bony point or protrusion. The hands should never leave the patient's back. Moving up the back, pressure is applied with the heels of the hands. On the downstroke, returning to the buttocks, the fingertips and the hand should lightly touch but not press.

Light massage for ten minutes at a time can be used as often as needed. Usually, two to four massages daily are adequate. Such massage is entirely harmless; it should be painless; and for spasm relaxation there is a valuable additive effect when the massage is carried out after a hot tub bath or heat application.

OTHER TYPES OF MASSAGE

In addition to light stroking massage which can be applied safely and effectively at home by almost anyone without experience, there are other types which require skill and training and are best done by professionals.

An intermediate type of rubbing stroke, which is more often used in Europe than in this country, involves forming the hands into soft fists, and applying the backs of the first two joints of the fingers and the ball of each thumb. One hand goes on each side of the spine and is moved upward in a long, firm stroke.

Deep massage, using the heels of the hands, may be employed by a professional after some relaxation is first achieved with light stroking. For deep massage, the amount of pressure applied is much greater.

Several types of slapping or striking strokes also may be used by professionals. The principle behind such massage is that with slapping or striking, muscles tend to contract and then, subsequently, to relax more fully. The effect is somewhat similar to that of exercise.

In one type of striking stroke, the fingers of both hands are tapped onto the patient. This is achieved with the wrists held limp and the hands flicked. Another type of stroke which achieves the same effect is hacking; for this, the edges of the hands are brought down, not too forcefully, on the patient.

Slapping with the flat of the palm can be stinging and stimulating. Often used is a modification in which the palms are cupped and then slapped onto the back.

Still another massage maneuver consists of kneading or taking hold of a muscle and squeezing and even twisting it gently but firmly. Kneading is often helpful in relaxing large tense muscles.

Massage may also include passive movement—a gentle pulling and twisting of small joints and movement of arm and leg joints through their full range of motion, and turning of the head from side to side.

Two or more of these massage maneuvers may be used in combination. There are innumerable variations possible, too, in terms of tempo or rate of massage, pressure applied, and duration.

A skilled physical therapist has the knowledge and experience to choose the right kind of strokes for a particular patient. Usually, the therapist begins by applying heat to an affected area to help relax the muscles there. Depending upon individual need, the therapist may use a hot pack of towels for moist, superficial heat, or infrared lamps for dry, superficial heat; shortwave diathermy for deep heat penetration; or ultrasonic waves for still deeper penetration.

Massage, useful as it is, cannot stand alone. You may find that home massage accomplishes its purpose in relieving spasm and pain, but it is usually essential to go beyond, using other measures as well in order to obtain more complete relief, and to go still farther to correct the underlying problem that produces the spasm and pain.

Similarly, the massage given by a physical therapist is rarely if ever the sole measure used but is associated with other forms of therapy and with overall medical treatment.

Unfortunately many people, including backache sufferers, seek out commercial massage parlors, hoping for miraculous cures from massage alone.

IF PROFESSIONAL MASSAGE IS NEEDED

Massage parlors can be divided roughly into two types: sexy and straight. The sexy usually are easy enough to identify: women, often scantily attired, massage men. Some of these establishments, as noted, are really only slightly disguised places of prostitution.

Generally, the straight parlors offer steam and sauna baths along with massage. While heat is helpful for relaxation, sauna baths may be stressful and possibly dangerous for anyone with a heart or respiratory problem.

While some commercial masseurs are skilled, many may, quite literally, rub the wrong way for a person with a backache or other physical problem. Not all states have laws regulating massage. In some, it is possible for anyone to set himself up as a masseur and to proceed, without training or skill, to give back rubs. In other states, all masseurs are licensed. In still other states—New York is one—a dual system is in effect, with both licensed and unlicensed masseurs operating. The licensed (as the medical author well knows since he is Chairman of the New York State Board for Massage) undergo a rigorous 3,600-hour training program and must pass a licensing examination, which is quite difficult and tests for knowledge of anatomy, biology, neurology, physiology, pathology, hygiene, and first aid as well as massage techniques. Unlicensed masseurs may have some training but often have none beyond the experience of watching someone else do massage.

You can, of course, inquire of a masseur about his or her training; you may or may not get a satisfactory answer. City or state licensing authorities often can provide information.

Your physician may have knowledge of a good commercial massage establishment, and he, and the physical therapy department of your local hospital, may have a list of experienced physical therapists and masseurs.

CONNECTIVE TISSUE MASSAGE: A SPECIAL KIND

A different type of quite special massage, connective tissue massage, is widely used in Europe but much less so here, although we have used it with some good results at ICD.

It originated with Elizabeth Dicke, a German physiotherapist, who herself, in 1929, was suffering from an almost unbearable backache along with a disturbance of circulation in her right leg so severe that amputation had been suggested.

While lying on her side, she tried to obtain some relief for her back pain by stroking over the painful areas. So extremely sensitive were certain areas that even slight stroking with the fingertips provoked great pain. Yet, she noticed, gradually the pain in the back subsided after such stroking and was replaced by a pleasant sensation of warmth. After several more days of the stroking, some improvement seemed to be occurring in her leg, to the extent that a warm sensation replaced the previous sensation of coldness. With several more months of treatment by another physiotherapist who followed Mrs. Dicke's directions, both leg and back were markedly improved and Mrs. Dicke resumed her occupation as a physiotherapist.

It appears that certain other phenomena were associated with Mrs. Dicke's case. Reportedly, during the course of her illness, she had also experienced disturbances in internal organs: she suffered from gastritis, her liver showed enlargement, and kidney function was disturbed. There were also symptoms suggestive of angina pectoris, the chest pain associated with impairment of circulation to the heart muscle. These complaints seemed to clear up simultaneously with improvement in the back and in the leg.

It seemed to Mrs. Dicke that certain body surface areas were associated with certain internal organs. Investigations by several German physicians suggested that there might be something to this. Out of such work carried on in the 1930's there grew up a method, called *Bindegewebsmassage* in Germany, which is used there and in other European countries for a variety of internal disorders.

Actually, at the turn of the century, an English neurologist, Head, had reported finding that abnormal changes in internal organs are accompanied by changes in the skin areas that have the same nerve supply as the internal organs. Later, some investigators reported finding changes in muscles as well—muscles that, like the skin areas, have the same nerve supply as the internal organs.

Mrs. Dicke is credited by the supporters of connective tissue massage with discovering that abnormal changes can also take place in subcutaneous tissue, which lies between skin and muscle.

The skin, of course, is the outermost layer of body tissues and contains specialized nerve endings sensitive to touch and temperature. Muscles can be looked upon as the deepest layer of tissues forming the body surface, and they, too, contain many nerve endings—these sensitive to changes in the length of muscle fibers.

Connective tissue is widely distributed throughout the body, surrounding blood vessels and nerves, forming sheaths around muscles, providing support for muscles and nerves, and serving as a connecting link between structures.

Proponents of connective tissue massage acknowledge that it is still impossible to account for all its reported effects, although there is a theory that it may act to stimulate the parasympathetic nervous system.

The parasympathetic system is part of the second great network of nerves in the body known as the autonomic system. The first network, of course, is the well-known central nervous system, which includes the brain and provides for voluntary control of activities. On the other hand, the autonomic system, with branches connecting to the heart, blood vessels, and various organs including those of the gastrointestinal and urinary tracts, provides for functions that can be carried out with no conscious thought. As its name implies, it is automatic.

And it is a system of checks and balances. It is, in fact, made up of two opposing systems, sympathetic and parasympathetic. As examples of how these work: while the sympathetic system dilates the pupils of the eyes, the parasympathetic constricts them; and while the sympathetic speeds the heartbeat, the parasympathetic slows it.

The autonomic system is influenced strongly by emotions. When, for example, you experience goose pimples and a dry mouth because of fear, the autonomic system is at work and, in this case, the sympathetic part of the system is in the ascendancy.

In times of stress, the sympathetic system takes over because stress—to the body—represents danger. The sympathetic system can ready the body to meet the danger. It dilates the pupils of the eyes so vision is optimal for fighting or fleeing; it can stop the activities of kidneys and excretory organs because fleeing or fighting is more important in the presence of stress, or so it seems, than waste elimination. It can stop digestive activities because they, too, seem of lesser importance. It can increase the heart rate so more blood is pumped, and it can direct more of the blood to the muscles, which need it for fighting or fleeing, by reducing the flow to the skin.

All this is fine for real emergencies—and once an emergency is over, the parasympathetic system can go to work and counter the previous activities of the sympathetic system to the point where normal body functions are resumed.

But if an individual is under virtually chronic stress, if almost always he or she has a stress (fight or flee) stance with muscles tensed for action, the muscles can go into spasm, and there may be repercussions elsewhere in any one or several body organs.

Therefore, stimulation of the parasympathetic nervous system—to "cool" the body down—could be helpful. And the theory has it that connective tissue massage somehow manages to achieve that.

In connective tissue massage, the third, fourth, and fifth fingers are used, and the fingernails must be so short that they never touch the skin. A roll of skin is pulled along in front of the fingers.

The massage, whenever possible, is carried out with the patient in the seated position, although it can be done, when necessary, with the patient lying down. The therapist sits behind and below the patient, usually on a special stool.

The strokes start in the pelvic area and usually, but not always, are from the midline out. A special series of strokes is used around the rhomboid of Michaelis, a diamond-shaped area formed by the two dimples, one on either side of the low back, the coccyx (which is the bone right in the crease of the buttocks), and a midline point above the dimples. "Hooking" motions are used around the iliac or pelvic bone and over it, and then there is a progression of massage up the back.

In a tense patient, connective tissue massage often produces the feeling that the flesh is being cut by a knife even though only the soft tissues are pressed upon by the fingers. One result of the massage is dilation of blood vessels and consequent reddening of the skin. On occasion, in some sensitive individuals, wheals are raised and may itch. Because connective tissue massage may cause the heart to race, it should not be used for patients with heart disease or severe hypertension unless a physician is present.

As we have already noted, some fervent proponents of the technique have claimed that it is of value in many internal disorders. Whether there is any validity to these claims is not something we have investigated at ICD. But we have had a number of years of experience with the technique in patients with back pain.

We have used it for as many as ten patients a day and with great success, especially in those who have been extremely tense with a great deal of muscle spasm which has not been adequately overcome by other measures. We are not certain of all that the technique accomplishes. We do know that muscle spasm is relieved even when the spasm has become chronic and when fibromyositic adhesions are present in muscle groups and between skin and muscles. Strangely, although it is an extremely stimulating type of massage, relaxation afterward is extraordinary.

Beneficial effects may persist for months after a series of treatments. A single connective tissue massage treatment is of little value. At least ten to twenty treatments may be required before any significant improvement occurs.

Only a very few skilled physical therapists and masseurs in this country are familiar with the technique. Information about those qualified to use it may be obtained from the American Physical Therapy Association, 1740 Broadway, New York, N.Y., the physical therapy department of a local hospital, or the licensing agency of the state.

Connective tissue massage has been claimed to help severe vascular (blood vessel) disease. There is a body of evidence indicating that patients with peripheral vascular disease benefit to some extent. The massage does dilate blood vessels, often to a greater degree than body heating, which is often a useful measure.

We see many patients at ICD with peripheral vascular disease, and connective tissue massage has occasionally been helpful in improving the vascular supply of the legs, especially in patients with arteriosclerosis associated with diabetes. No type of treatment presently available reverses the arteriosclerotic process. But measures to dilate blood vessels may help improve leg circulation for patients with vascular disease and, in so doing, may delay or avoid need for amputation.

ZONE THERAPY

Because it makes use of pressure application, zone therapy can be considered a form of massage. But it is also somewhat akin to acupuncture because it is based on the concept that there are segments in the body—in effect, channels connecting various parts of the body—and that pressure stimulation in one area may have beneficial effects in another far-removed area.

The concept is not new and zone therapy is not new. To a large extent, the therapy has been relegated to obscurity because of the many, many claims made for it. Yet on occasion zone therapy does appear to be useful in relieving back pain; and it is a therapy that can be tried at home.

Proponents of zone therapy have pointed out that all of us practice a kind of laying on of hands, with some pressure, when we hurt ourselves. If we bump against a door, we rub the bumped spot. The rubbing has a soothing influence. Moreover, zone therapy proponents suggest, pressure applied to an injury may produce pressure on nerves running from the injured site to the brain, cutting off the flow of impulses and reducing or eliminating the awareness of pain.

According to the original theory of zone therapy, pressure, if properly applied, can do much more. The body, the theory holds, is divided longitudinally into ten zones, five on each side of a median line. On each side, the five zones begin in the toes and end in the thumb and fingers, so that the first zone, for example, extends from the great toe up the entire height of the body from front to back, across chest and back, to the head, and down the arm into the thumb.

And the theory holds that pain in any part of the first zone may be treated and overcome—at least temporarily and often permanently—by pressure on the first joint of the great toe or the corresponding joint of the thumb.

Zone therapy enthusiasts, and they have included some physicians, have claimed that it is possible, through application of pressure to specific areas, to relieve headaches, earaches, toothaches, painful conditions of the throat, bronchitis, asthma, hay fever, rheumatism, neuralgia, nausea, and much more. But convincing scientific proof of the validity of such claims has not been produced. Nor has there ever been any satisfactory explanation of how, if it is effective, zone therapy really works.

Nevertheless, while we have no confidence in the theory or in the proposed zone distribution, we have found that sometimes zone therapy is useful for back pain. Perhaps it works through suggestion, or through counterirritation, or through some nervous reflex mechanism not presently understood, but severe pressure sometimes does provide relief.

A typical zone therapy treatment may consist of squeezing either the fingers or the toes—on their lateral as well as front and back sides—as hard as possible for about thirty seconds. Sometimes, fingers may be wrapped tightly with a rubber band for a short period. (A rubber band should never be left in place for more than two minutes because of the danger of complete interruption of blood flow.) Sometimes, clothespins may be used to compress the fingers.

For back pain, we have found that a metal comb, such as used for grooming a dog, can be employed. The teeth of the comb are pressed firmly to the palm of the hand and the palmar surfaces of thumb, first, second, and third fingers. The pressure can be continued for ten to twenty minutes. Sometimes it is also useful to apply the comb pressure to the web spaces between thumb and index finger and between index and middle fingers. The comb may also be used to stimulate the soles of the feet.

At home, one can use any type of pressure—applied by hand, spring clothespin, rubber band, or comb—on the palmar surfaces of the hands and on the first, second, and third fingers, or on the thumb, index, and middle fingers. The pressure should be applied for five to twenty minutes, except for rubber band pressure, which should be limited to two minutes.

It is impossible to predict accurately whether zone therapy will have any effect whatever in an individual case, but since it is not dangerous, it is feasible to try and see whether it can relieve spasm and pain if other measures do not provide adequate relief. If any benefit is at all likely to be obtained, you should notice some by the fifth treatment, and if there is some benefit you can then repeat the treatment as often as necessary.

If you are going to have someone else stimulate your feet, pressure should be applied—with a comb or the blunt end of a ballpoint pen—to the great toe and the two adjacent toes. The pressure should be as great as you can stand and should be applied for five minutes to each toe and the adjacent portions of the soles. If pressure is applied to both hands and feet five times without any benefit, the treatment should be discontinued as ineffective for you.

Many patients treated with zone therapy at ICD and some who have used the technique at home have reported great benefit.

One of our interesting cases was that of a longshoreman with very severe back pain which was not responding to other measures. He was seen at ICD just at the point when we were first considering the possibility of trying zone therapy for recalcitrant cases. We had no great confidence in the technique. Not even a metal comb was available.

We simply tried applying thumb pressure to the ball of his great toe (on the foot on the side where he had the greatest amount of back muscle spasm). The patient complained increasingly of the pain in the toe from the pressure and finally sat up on the table complaining that he could take no more of it. He had not been able to sit up or make any other move as rapidly as that for the past week, and after he stopped storming about his aching toe, he suddenly realized that his back pain was gone.

For him, the relief lasted for about a day before the pain slowly began to return. But other measures then could be used to maintain the pain relief and relaxation of spasm, permitting us to get on with a corrective program for him.

Zone therapy, as we have indicated, cannot be counted on to work invariably. Nor, certainly, is it invariably needed. We must also emphasize that even when it does work, other measures, such as heat and massage, usually are needed to maintain the relaxation of muscle spasm. All of these measures are at best only palliative. It is important to relieve spasm and pain—for once the relief is obtained, much can be done to correct the problems that produced the spasm and pain in the first place.

CHAPTER 8

MANIPULATION

The victim hobbles into the office and his agony is obvious. During the course of the examination, he is asked to bend forward. He tries but comes to a painful stop before his fingers even reach knee level. He is then helped onto a table, his spine is manipulated briefly, whereupon he utters a great sigh of relief, gets up from the table on his own, walks without his previous list, and is able to bend to within eight inches of the floor without discomfort.

The scene is not, as one might expect, the office of a chiropractor but rather of a physician.

Manipulation is emerging from the shadows. More and more physicians now employ it in treating back disorders. A professional society, the North American Academy of Manipulative Medicine, has been organized by American and Canadian physicians to carry out, and to encourage others to carry out, scientific studies of manipulation.

While manipulation is a useful tool in approaching certain problems, it is certainly no panacea. It has long been in the shadows because of its ill-advised, widespread, often indiscriminate use by practitioners without medical training to treat people with a wide variety of conditions. Perhaps wrongfully, many physicians in the past wanted nothing whatever to do with it because of its disrepute; it might have been better all around if medicine many years ago had paid serious attention to it and to exploring its possibilities and marking out clearly the boundaries for its use. At any rate, that effort is being made now.

It has sometimes seemed that everyone wanted to get into the manipulation business. Osteopaths have made some use of it. Chiropractors, of course, make very large use of it. But manipulation has been practiced, too, by some steam-bath attendants, "health" club therapists, ex-boxers, ex-wrestlers, physical directors, trainers, and masseurs.

Osteopathic medicine has been defined as a system of therapy based on the theory that the body is capable of making its own remedies against disease and other toxic conditions when it is in normal structural relationship and has favorable environmental conditions and adequate nutrition. While placing considerable emphasis on the importance of normal body mechanics and manipulative methods of detecting and correcting faulty structure, osteopathic medicine uses generally accepted physical, medicinal, and surgical methods of diagnosis and therapy.

Chiropractic, started in 1895 by D. D. Palmer of Davenport, Iowa, a grocer turned "magnetic healer," has been defined as a system of therapeutics based upon the claim that disease is caused by abnormal function of the nervous system. It attempts to restore normal function of the nervous system by manipulation and treatment of the structures of the body, especially the spinal column.

According to chiropractic theory, subluxations and dislocations of vertebrae cause pressure upon nerves, leading to diminished resistance to disease and to the appearance of abnormal conditions. A dislocation is a separation of the two sides of a joint surface, usually with tearing of the joint capsule. A sub-luxation is a partial separation of joint surfaces.

It should be clear to even the most poorly read individual that, for example, tuberculosis is caused by the tuberculosis germ and poliomyelitis by a specific transmissible virus. While manipulation may occasionally offer some relief and comfort to patients with various diseases, there is no doubt that most people with tuberculosis today would not consent to being treated by manipulation alone but would want treatment with medications known to combat the tuberculosis organisms.

No one with any extensive experience in treating back pain will deny that manipulation may be useful under some conditions. Not all backache can be helped by it; none can be cured by it—whether the manipulation is chiropractic or medical.

The basic difference between chiropractic and medical manipulation is not so much in manipulative technique as in conditions of use. While osteopathic and medical physicians have many methods of diagnosis and treatment to use, the chiropractor, by law and by training, has only the one. If manipulation is what is really needed, chiropractic manipulation may have value. If manipulation is not needed, chiropractic manipulation not only may be of no value but may be a serious disservice. Unfortunately, much of the advertising for chiropractic implies that virtually all diseases can be treated by it. To be sure, any method including manipulation can be used to "treat" a disease. Cancer can be "treated" by manipulation—but not with success. Unfortunately, manipulation, by providing some measure of temporary relief, may mask a serious condition that needs an entirely different form of therapy.

Manipulation involves the movement of bones to alter their relationships. And when, indeed, there has been subluxation or dislocation of a joint, manipulation can be valuable.

For a normal joint to subluxate or dislocate, there must of necessity have been stretching of periarticular structures—that is, those structures such as ligaments that surround the joint. A joint may subluxate or dislocate because the surrounding structures were loose to begin with, perhaps congenitally (as in the double-jointed) or as the result of some previous injury. Or a sudden acute injury may produce the subluxation or dislocation. A common cause of such injury is bending or lifting in a quick, uncoordinated, jerky fashion. Once surrounding structures become stretched, the joint surfaces themselves can move out of normal relationship with each other, and the pain may be severe.

The purpose of manipulation then is to stretch the surrounding tissues enough to unlock the joint and permit the joint surfaces to be returned to their normal relationship. Often, when this is done, there is immediate, dramatic relief of pain, for when subluxation or dislocation occurs, so does muscle spasm. The spasm serves as a splint around the affected joint and is meant for protection but produces pain in due course. When the subluxation or dislocation is overcome by manipulation, the spasm is also reduced.

Manipulation also may be used to purposely subluxate or dislocate a joint temporarily when the problem lies with a contracted, scarred joint capsule and adhesions. When this condition is present, joint motion produces pain as adhesions are pulled upon. If the adhesions are torn by sudden manipulation, the normal range of joint motion may be restored and there may be immediate pain relief.

Manipulation sometimes may have value in degenerative disk disease if the extruded nucleus pulposus, which is causing pain by pressure on a nerve root, can be broken off cleanly and then moves away from the nerve root so pressure is eliminated. There is some risk, however, that the material may not break off and pressure on the nerve root may even be increased.

Manipulation of the upper back—in the cervical, or neck, region—carries more risk than does manipulation of the low back, for the spinal cord ends just under the first lumbar vertebra, slightly below where the lowest rib comes off. Thus, manipulation in the low back cannot influence the spinal cord. In the cervical region, the spinal cord is present in the spinal canal and there is little room between cord and spinal bones. There have been some cases of paralysis after improper cervical manipulation. Cervical manipulation can be useful when properly done, but the risks must be borne in mind.

In manipulation, one side of a joint is stabilized and the other is moved against it. For example, a patient will lie supine, his right shoulder held down by the manipulator's left hand. The right side of the pelvis may be rotated as far to the patient's left as possible, taking up the slack in the joint. The manipulator may then use his right hand to press downward toward the patient's left on the back of the iliac crest and then may make a sudden sharp thrust downward to separate the locked joint surfaces and click them over each other.

A manipulative treatment may require no more than a minute or two, and if successful, no repetition is needed. In some cases, the treatment period may be longer if there is need for relaxing muscle spasm first in order to allow adequate manipulative movement.

Is there any way you can tell whether manipulation might be helpful in your case? One possible clue is if your back pain came on instantly after some sudden movement, especially if you heard or felt a sudden snap. That could suggest subluxation or dislocation, which might benefit from manipulation. Remember, however, that not every sudden backache is necessarily due to either subluxation or dislocation; much more frequently, a sprain is involved.

An additional clue, if the pain did come on after a sudden movement, lies in whether or not rest increases joint stiffness and pain or provides some relief. If the symptoms improve with rest, there is added likelihood that manipulation may help. If rest only accentuates the symptoms, something besides subluxation or dislocation may be involved, and manipulation should not be used until this possibility is investigated.

Manipulation can be carried out with or without anesthesia. Generally, it is safer without anesthesia, which removes the protective elements of muscle spasm and pain. But, when necessary, with proper precautions, anesthesia can be used to permit manipulation that might otherwise not be possible.

If you think manipulative treatment may be helpful for you, you should seek out a physician who is expert in its use. Orthopedic surgeons and physicians who specialize in physical medicine and rehabilitation are knowledgeable, and your family physician or local medical society can provide the names of several. All osteopathic physicians are skilled in manipulation. Our emphatic recommendation is that you seek out either an osteopathic or knowledgeable medical physician or surgeon rather than a chiropractor, since if you have a condition not amenable to manipulative treatment, a physician or surgeon will be able to determine what the real problem is and can treat it without delay.

It is vitally important to consider manipulation in its proper place. It is useful in many cases. It is of no value and may even be harmful in others. Moreover, when it is useful, it is not to be considered as the sole treatment. It cannot be relied upon in and of itself.

The reason is simple. Any dislocation or subluxation means that the joint capsule and surrounding structures have been stretched. Without such stretching the dislocation or subluxation could not have occurred.

When manipulation is performed, the structures are stretched once again to permit normal structural relationships to be restored. But the structures, after stretching, do not spring back immediately as does a rubber band.

If, after manipulation, the structures are permitted to remain in normal relationship, then over the course of several weeks they will gradually contract and resume their normal distance from each other, and this will help to maintain the integrity of the joint for an extended period and possibly permanently.

On the other hand, if the structures are not given the chance to resume normal length, another subluxation or dislocation may occur. This may be treated again by manipulation. As more and more manipulations are performed, more and more stretching of the structures occurs, and the need for still more manipulation may be increased. There is then a vicious cycle of subluxation or dislocation, stretching, further subluxation or dislocation, and more stretching.

Manipulation, if used as the sole therapeutic tool without suitable aftercare, thus tends to perpetuate its own need. After manipulation, movement should be so restricted that there is no chance for the previously subluxated or dislocated joint to go beyond its normal range of motion.

When musculature is adequate, then in most cases the patient can be instructed in using muscles in a coordinated manner to protect against repeated subluxation or dislocation. With proper coordination and adequately strong muscles, excessive joint motion can be avoided and stretched structures can be given the chance to return to normal length.

In some cases, it may be necessary to resort to a corset or brace for a period of four to six weeks. There are rare cases for which surgical treatment may be needed because of constantly recurring subluxation or dislocation. Bone fusion may be needed or capsular structures may have to be tied to tighten them; the tying, in effect, is simliar to taking in clothes which have become too large.

TRACTION

An integral part of the manipulative procedure is drawing or pulling, which is traction. Traction alone, if continued for a sufficient period of time, can accomplish the same end result as manipulation. It is generally safer than manipulation and stretches the joint structures less.

It amounts to this: If one has a subluxated or dislocated joint, the surfaces may be pulled apart suddenly by manipulation and then allowed to slip back into normal relationship, or a traction force may be applied to cause the muscles gently to "give" until the joint surfaces come apart and then, when traction is stopped, the surfaces can slip together into normal relationship.

The principle behind traction is that after a time when they are being pulled upon, muscles fatigue, relax, and allow stretching of joint structures. Traction force can be applied so that the pull not only allows stretching but is directed so that it helps to align the joints so they can pop more readily back into proper relationship when traction is ended.

Traction can be used for both low back and cervical area problems. There is less danger of injury, especially in the cervical area.

As often used at home or in the hospital, traction employs no more than 15 pounds of pull and may do little more than serve as a means of assuring more complete rest for an area of the spine. The traction we are discussing here for back problems is heavy traction, using from 15 to as much as 200 pounds of pull for the lower back and from 5 to 40 pounds for the neck region. Many physicians do not use more than 20 pounds for cervical traction, but at ICD we have used 45 and even 50 pounds without harm.

Traction may be either constant or intermittent. For the low back, we have used up to 200 pounds of intermittent traction with excellent results. I (the medical author) remember the particular instance that started me on use of such traction. The medical director under whom I served when I first came to ICD had just ordered a pelvic traction table capable of intermittent traction of up to 200 pounds. I had never seen such a device used and I remarked, rather presumptuously, to the director: "You've just wasted $3,000 on that machine. It's garbage." The director shrugged and said: "Maybe. But I want to try it." Over the next year, he did—a number of times and with seeming success.

But I did not use it until one day when I had a 36-year-old construction worker with severe low back pain and with pain radiating down the right leg. I had used just about every method I could think of to try to help him—all without success. Finally, in desperation, I decided to try the "piece of garbage." Fifteen minutes after I put the patient on the traction table, he told me that he was free of pain. The heavy traction was more effective than the manipulation I had tried because my manipulation did not relax this man's enormously developed musculature sufficiently to relocate the subluxated joint.

There is considerable difference, obviously, between using such heavy traction and using light amounts not great enough to overcome the enormous forces that can be applied by the back muscles. While light amounts of traction are effective over a period of time in fatiguing and stretching muscles elsewhere —in the neck or extremities, for example—the enormously strong muscles of the back cannot be stretched by as small a weight as 10 or 15 pounds. But this is the maximum one can use in bed, since greater pull may succeed only in pulling the patient toward the foot of the bed.

A special type of traction apparatus is required for pulls of up to 200 pounds. It also applies stabilizing countertraction by means of a series of straps around the chest. The heavy traction is generally applied by another set of straps around the iliac crests or the hip bones. The treatment usually lasts half an hour with alternate traction and relaxation during that time.

Other types of traction apparatus only provide up to 100 pounds of pull, but some of them are capable of providing constant traction.

At home, if other measures such as rest, heat, massage, counterirritants, and analgesics are not enough, traction can be tried. It enforces rest when used for the low back. When applied to the neck region, it separates the vertebrae, takes pressure off nerve roots, and relaxes spasm. A pelvic or cervical traction set can be obtained from a pharmacy or surgical supply store. Some extra back traction can be applied if blocks, six to nine inches in height, are placed under the foot of the bed so as to tilt the head down. In this way, body weight provides some countertraction. Even then, only 15 to 20 pounds of traction is usually feasible.

Cervical traction is excellent for neck and upper back pain, especially for pain due to degenerative disk disease in the neck area. As we have noted, cervical traction is far safer than

manipulation. At ICD we almost never use cervical manipulation because of the possibility of occasional adverse consequences, but we use cervical traction often.

Cervical traction may be applied in either supine or sitting position. Generally, patients prefer sitting. The traction may be intermittent or constant. Home treatment is best carried out with a system that has two pulleys attached to a metal frame which hooks over a door. A head halter is used. It is most important that traction be applied with the neck bent downward 15 to 20 degrees or even more. Traction done with the neck extended or straight up may increase pain. The face should be oriented toward the chest and the eyes should be looking at something on the floor rather than straight ahead.

Recently, plastic bags that can be filled with ordinary tap water have become available for use as weights. They have lines indicating how much they weigh when filled with water to various levels.

Traction should be used for 20 to 30 minutes, two or three times a day. One can spend the time reading.

Generally, traction should be employed only on advice of a physician—usually after an x-ray has been taken of the neck area to assure that none of the rare conditions that might be aggravated by cervical traction are present.

If heavy traction is needed for a low back problem, most specialists in physical medicine and rehabilitation have the necessary equipment in their offices, as do some orthopedic surgeons and many physical therapists.

CHAPTER 9

OTHER PHYSICAL THERAPIES

AND MEASURES

ELECTRICAL STIMULATION

Although much attention has gone into finding ways to overcome muscle spasm, since this is such a common feature of back pain, one excellent spasm-relief measure, electrical stimulation, is not used as often as it should be.

Sometimes capable of providing relief even when hot and cold applications, massage, and other measures have failed, electrical stimulation causes muscles in spasm to contract even more than they are already doing in spasm.

The principle is simple: If a muscle is contracted in spasm and will not let go, it may let go and relax if it is stimulated to the point of fatigue and exhaustion. Electrical stimulation can be applied continuously to produce tetany, or constant muscle contraction. Or it may be applied sinusoidally—in waves—forcing the muscle to build up to a crescendo of contraction.

Electrical stimulation is not usually considered to be practical for home use. For one thing, the equipment is too costly for use, under ordinary circumstances, by just one person. The equipment is so designed that when properly maintained, as it can be when used frequently by professional personnel, there is no danger of shock. Moreover, when electrical stimulation is carried out by a trained person—physician, nurse, or physical therapist—it is likely to be more effective.

Why electrical stimulation is so little used is something of a mystery. One might expect that every physician treating many backache patients, and certainly every major institution, would have electrical stimulation equipment. That isn't the case in actuality; yet if you are plagued with muscle spasm that has not been adequately relieved by other measures, you should be able to find electrical stimulation therapy available somewhere nearby.

In use, electrical stimulation comes as a pleasant surprise for many people. A common expectation is that an electrical current applied to the body must have a kind of jolting effect, but electrical stimulation in reality is so comfortable and relaxing that most patients fall asleep while it is applied.

Because it seems to have a central nervous system sedative effect in addition to its direct effect on spasmodic muscles, there is some speculation that electrical stimulation may have something in common with Chinese acupuncture anesthesia (in which electrical impulses are channeled through acupuncture needles) and with Russian electrosleep therapy (in which electrical impulses are fed through electrodes applied to the head).

Electrical stimulation is applied through pads, generally two to four inches square, soaked in plain water or in a solution to promote electrical conduction. Two to four of the pads may be used and held firmly on the back by weights so that even, well-distributed contact is maintained. The current—either alternating or direct may be used—is small, usually in a range up to 50 milliampheres, or thousandths of an ampere.

An electrical stimulation session usually lasts for about ten minutes, and although at the beginning some slight pinprick sensations may be felt, these usually disappear rapidly.

The medical author must confess to being greatly enamored of certain vigorous activities such as horseback riding and skiing—and, unfortunately, these are also activities which may involve occasional minor injuries and consequent muscle spasm, to which I am still not immune. I am in the fortunate position, however, whenever afflicted, of being able immediately upon reaching the office next morning to walk into the physical therapy department for ten minutes of electrical stimulation to relax the spasm. With a bit of massage added on, I can work the rest of the day without discomfort.

Electrical stimulation is so useful that at ICD it is used almost routinely for any patient with severe muscle spasm. To be sure, there is the occasional extremely high-strung, nervous individual who does not give electrical stimulation a chance; his or her fear is so great that we have to discontinue the treatment, but this is extremely rare.

Abnormal fear of electrical currents aside, there is one contraindication to electrical stimulation. In the rare person who has no skin sensation, the treatment should not be used—nor, in fact, should diathermy or hot packs—because of the possibility of burns.

Some children tolerate electrical stimulation well. Others may be frightened. But if stimulation is applied first to the mother or to the therapist and a game is made of its use, many children come to tolerate it well.

At ICD, therapists frequently combine the two types of electrical stimulation, using continuous tetanizing stimulation first, then surging sinusoidal stimulation. We have found that occasionally the deep fibers in large muscles are not adequately stimulated by currents until the superficial fibers have become fatigued. Continuous stimulation tends to fatigue the more superficial fibers most effectively, while the surging type relaxes some of the deeper ones when used after the continuous stimulation.

FOR MORE RESTFUL SLEEP

A common complaint of backache sufferers is increased discomfort in the morning. Upon awakening, they experience stiffness and their first movements may be excruciatingly painful, with some easing of the pain later as they "loosen up."

The stiffness is related to lack of adequate motion during the night. If motion during sleep is severely limited, there may be some "gelling" of body proteins, reduction of blood and lymphatic circulation, and thickening of joint fluid.

All of us are aware of the urge to stretch after any prolonged period of sitting still. Stretching appears to be a response to a body need for moving muscles and joints at least occasionally to prevent stiffness.

We are aware now, too—thanks to the intensive research that has gone into studying the whole process of sleeping—that we do not normally fall into bed and sleep "like a log," making no movement during the night. On the contrary, much is going on while we sleep. We go through various stages and depths of sleep; in one stage, which is related to dreaming, the eyes make rapid movements, as rapid as any they make when we are awake. And, during the night, there is much body movement, much twisting and turning—or should be.

For good sleep, reparative and restorative, certain conditions appear to be essential. The surface on which we stretch out must allow easy motion, and it must also allow the body, and especially the back, to rest in a favorable position. For the back, the best position is one that produces least strain, and that is the position in which the spine is relatively straight so that there is neither excessive flexion nor excessive extension.

The fact is that many back patients have discovered for themselves that sleeping on a rug on the floor may be much more comfortable for them than sleeping in a bed. A firm surface helps to assure that the back will not assume strained positions, and it also eases movement during the night.

An inexpensive, old-fashioned, two- or three-inch-high horsehair mattress, to which we have referred earlier, is excellent for back sufferers when used on a bedboard without springs, since it provides support where needed and permits easy movement.

Support, if sleeping is done in supine position, should be provided for heels, thighs, buttocks, and the back (at the level of the chest), allowing maintenance of the normal hollow in the low back. If a pillow is used when sleeping supine, it should be a very low pillow. If one habitually sleeps on the side, a thicker pillow should be used to support the head so it does not drop below the shoulder.

Some people sleep comfortably in prone position; others do not. For backache sufferers, the prone or "on the stomach" sleeping position is not recommended, since it tends to extend and strain the back.

There are proponents, especially commercial ones, of "even pressure." They have developed ways to provide such even pressure distribution for the back. One of these is the waterbed.

Some patients with back pain report that they find the waterbed of some value. Yet, turning in a waterbed is difficult. In addition to being expensive, waterbeds are heavy, and some old buildings cannot support their weight. The major advertising point for the waterbed usually is not that it is particularly helpful for backache but rather that is is, supposedly, helpful for sexual activities. For some patients with back pain who have difficulty with intercourse, this may be an attractive claim.

A newer device is the mud bed. It combines a special type of soil with water, is almost but not quite as heavy as the water-bed, and in the opinion of the authors is better than a waterbed for the person with back pain, since it makes turning easier and reduces the likelihood of morning stiffness.

An inexpensive alternative is to buy a $17 air mattress and partially fill it with water. It weighs only 250 pounds and some back patients find it helpful.

But for most backache victims we return to what we believe to be a better investment—of perhaps $20 for a horsehair mattress and $5 for a plywood bedboard. No springs should be used between board and mattress. If a horsehair mattress is unobtainable, a one- or two-inch firm foam rubber pad over a plywood board on top of a present mattress or directly on top of springs can be used.

Any rigid board can serve as a bedboard. The simplest and least expensive is made of plywood, generally three eighths to three quarters of an inch thick. You can buy a suitable sheet of plywood at a lumber yard, and the yard probably will cut it to desired dimensions. The board should be the size of the bedsprings so it will be supported by rigid steel along the outer perimeter of the bedsprings.

If you do much traveling, you will find that many of the larger hotels and motels have bedboards available on request. You can also buy a lightweight, folding bedboard to carry with you.

More than three fourths of back patients we see at ICD use bedboards on our recommendation—and it is interesting to note that spouses of the patients actually come to prefer sleeping on the boards after a short period of acclimatization.

Sometimes, during an acute back attack, assuming a more or less seated position in bed may be helpful. This can be achieved by placing a chair on its back on and at the foot of the bed, with the chair legs pointed toward the head of the bed. Lying supine, with hips and knees at 90 degrees, you can place your legs on a pillow supported by the legs and rungs of the chair. This position, which puts the back into kyphosis and reduces lordosis, is comfortable, especially during an acute back-pain episode, and is much like the position that can be achieved with a hospital bed.

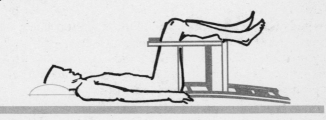

Under ordinary circumstances, one should sleep in the position that is most comfortable. And, given a suitable sleeping surface which provides for proper support and allows ready movement, the individual will, almost automatically, find what is for him the most comfortable basic position and will automatically, too, change positions during the night so as to maintain comfort and avoid stiffness.

There are additional measures that may be helpful for avoiding morning stiffness and pain. Long-acting aspirins are available, and two tablets taken at bedtime may provide for a pain-free awakening. So may application of a counterirritant (a greaseless, stainless one) at bedtime.

Be sure to use a warm cover, even in summer. An electric blanket is comforting; it should be used at low heat. Drafts from an air conditioner or fan should be avoided. Some people want to have an air conditioner blow directly at them, especially when they sleep. Although the mechanism is not known, cold drafts can sometimes lead to muscle spasm and trigger-point formation.

SITTING

A good sitting position—both at work and during periods of relaxation—is important. The best basic position is one with hips and knees at right angles and feet flat on the floor.

Sitting erect is desirable, and for this there must be adequate support for the back so that the lordotic curve in the low back can be maintained without muscular effort. A good chair with a properly shaped back can provide for this.

If a secretarial chair is used, it should have a movable back section that permits adjustment to individual need. The height of the seat also should be adjustable.

LIFTING

Dr. Erwin Tischauer, of New York University, has carried out extensive studies of back pain in industry and its relationship to lifting. He has demonstrated that lifting a *small*, light package is easy, but lifting a package that is no heavier but is larger in dimensions may be difficult because the center of gravity of the package is far in front of the body—difficult enough so that it is a frequent cause of back pain.

When lifting and carrying any package in front of you, it should be held as close to the body as possible. If a package is irregularly shaped, it should be held so that its longest dimension runs from side to side in front of you, the next longest dimension runs up and down, and the shortest extends ahead of you, thus allowing you to bring the package's weight center as close as possible to you.

When you carry a package at your side in one hand, its longest dimension should be from front to back and its shortest should be from your side out laterally, thus bringing its weight center in close.

All weight should be braced against the body. In lifting, there should be no bending from the waist. Instead, keep the back erect, bend with knees and hips prior to lifting, and make the lifting process predominantly one of straightening knees and hips with no use of the back at all.

CORSETS AND BRACES

Corsets and braces are sometimes of value for back patients.

There are instances in which bracing may be essential. After a severe injury to the spine, a brace—such as a Jewett hyperextension brace, a cumbersome contrivance extending from just above the pubic bone to below the base of the neck—may be a must. In cases in which back muscles have become paralyzed, a brace to support the spine may be unavoidable. Patients with scoliosis often need a special type of brace, called a "Milwaukee brace," which is designed to help correct spinal curvature; and, indeed, the Milwaukee brace is a valuable, conservative tool that may avoid need for surgery for scoliosis correction.

But in most cases of back pain, a brace is not needed. If support is required, a simpler, lighter, less costly corset is to be preferred.

A corset can act as a substitute for inadequate stomach musculature. In some patients who are unable to strengthen stomach muscles through exercise because of a severe heart condition, hernia, or other contraindication, the corset may need to be worn permanently. Far more often, it can be a temporary aid, to be worn only until stomach muscle strengthening is achieved.

The corset must be made so that the lower abdominal part can be tightened to pull up the stomach muscles, support the internal organs, and overcome excessive lordosis of the back which so often accompanies weak stomach musculature.

Corsets, including those with rigid stays, can be fairly comfortable if they are properly contoured to the back. Flexible steel stays can also be used. The stays serve to prevent some motion of the back; they do not curtail all motion. Curving around the back, they add stiffness to the stiffness provided by the corset material.

A corset tends to ride up when the wearer sits down. For that reason, it should be cupped under the buttocks. It is usually advisable in the case of a woman wearer for the corset to have garter attachments to help prevent riding up. Sometimes, especially for men, a strap in the groin may be needed to avoid the riding up.

TRAVEL

It is often helpful for back-pain sufferers when traveling by plane to place one or more small pillows (they are usually readily available on planes) in the small of the back.

Short people who experience back pain while traveling by plane may find it helpful to carry with them an old, inexpensive piece of luggage to be placed on the floor to prop the feet up in case an adequate foot rest is not available.

Tall people may have trouble when traveling by plane, especially in the coach section, with inadequate leg room. Whenever possible, they should try to get an aisle seat so they can stretch their feet at least occasionally. Some extra leg room often can be found, too, in the first seat behind the front partition of a plane or the first behind an emergency exit. Patients with back pain should not hesitate to request such seats prior to boarding; flight personnel are usually helpful about this.

As often as possible during a plane flight, especially a long one, it's helpful for anyone, especially a back-pain sufferer, to get up and move about at least a bit, walking up and down the aisle even if no more than once.

And in car travel, stopping every half hour or so to get out and walk around even just briefly can be helpful.

Car seats are often softly sprung, and making a seat more rigid can make travel easier for a back-pain victim. A ventilated seat of the type used for summer driving provides some desirable rigidity. In addition, various other types of seating devices are available. The best, in the experience of the medical author, is the only type sold by one New York City store, Hammacher Schlemmer, and may be available elsewhere. While it is fairly expensive, it is worth its cost for anybody with recurrent back pain. It consists of a net-covered metal frame for the seat and a curved metal back frame. The amount of curvature can be regulated by a screw, and the entire back section slides up and down to permit positioning for best support of the back. In addition, a spring allows adjusting the back forward and backward.

If back pain begins to develop and a special device is not available, any kind of cushion or even rolled-up clothing used to support the lordotic curve of the back can help. For a car passenger with back pain, the front seat is often preferable, since there usually is less jouncing there and more room to stretch the legs. The rear seat occasionally is useful when back pain is so severe that sitting up is no longer tolerable. In that case, the patient can recline, with hips and knees flexed, and experiment to find the best position for relief.

When traveling, every effort should be made, if pain begins to develop, to cut it short. If it is possible to apply heat or a counterirritant, all to the good. Analgesics can be used. Just rubbing one's own back when it starts to hurt is of value. Getting up to stretch, do a few knee-bends, tilt from side to side, and "limber up" the back can help.

Remember that when back pain begins to develop, almost invariably it is because muscle spasm is developing. The earlier you catch the spasm, the less severe it is likely to become and the easier it may be to eliminate.

CHAPTER 10

THE RARE NEED

FOR SURGERY

Surgery has a place, but a limited one, in treating back pain. Although there is still a common notion that, sooner or later, if there is really to be any hope for definitive cure of back pain, surgery has to be done and everything else is mere palliation, that is far from being the fact. In the vast majority of patients with back pain, not only is surgery unnecessary; it would be totally useless.

We have already mentioned what stands out as perhaps the largest and most thorough study ever done to establish just how often surgery is really needed. Carried out by physicians of two universities, Columbia and New York, it covered 5,000 unselected back patients. One after the other, as they came in with their back complaints, they were included in the investigation. There was no picking and choosing. That large a number of unselected patients constitutes, by all odds, a representative sample of the general population of back-pain sufferers.

And of all these 5,000 patients—men and women, young and old—81 percent had back pain which, if something more than merely immediate relief was to be provided, if recurrences were to be prevented, called not for surgery but for exercises designed to strengthen critically weak muscles and for ways of making such exercises feasible.

Some of the remaining 19 percent, and only some, needed surgical treatment—but not invariably surgery of the back. Nor, in many cases, even where surgery was one possible measure was it the only potentially useful measure.

For example, a woman with pain low in the back, often extending into the buttocks, may have it because of a retroverted uterus. When a uterus is retroverted, its fundus or top portion, instead of facing toward the abdominal wall, is tilted backward. The tilting produces a tug on ligaments which may cause back pain. Surgery may be needed, but sometimes a pessary suffices.

Nor is surgery needed for men with benign prostatic disease which may cause low back and buttock pain. A prostate may become inflamed and enlarged because of infection or sexual problems. The enlarged gland causes pain and a sense of fullness with a dull ache in the back. Massage empties the gland and reduces the swelling, relieving the backache. If infection is present, antibiotic treatment can be used.

Surgery on the back may or may not be indicated even in cases of tumors of the spinal column. If a patient has a benign tumor in bone, it may be as excruciatingly painful as a malignant tumor. In some cases, surgery is required; in others, radiotherapy may be best; and even for some malignant tumors, chemotherapy may be advisable.

Even the herniated intervertebral disk, which has been blamed, often wrongly, for so much back pain, does not invariably require surgical treatment. When a herniated disk causes back pain, it is because of pressure on a nerve root. The pain, which can be excruciating while it lasts, does not generally last very long, since a completely compressed nerve becomes anesthetic. Even patients with severe herniation of an intervertebral disk occasionally get better because the extruded nucleus pulposus material from the disk breaks off and no longer presses on the nerve but instead floats freely within the dura, or sac, which covers spinal cord and nerve roots.

The only time surgery on the back itself may be essential is when pressure on a nerve root must be relieved to relieve intractable pain or to halt progressive nerve damage and paralysis, or when there is painful motion in the spinal column which must be stopped to prevent pain recurrence.

Most of the time, pain from nerve root compression is not intractable provided proper measures such as traction, rest, and muscle-spasm-relieving procedures are used, but there are a few cases in which pain cannot be relieved within a reasonable period of time without surgery. In such cases, a procedure called laminectomy is used.

Laminectomy involves removal of part of the bony ring around the spinal sac to get at and remove the herniated disk material which is pressing on the nerve root. Usually, too, during the procedure, the intervertebral foramen—the hole through which the nerve passes—is enlarged so as to make it unlikely that there can ever again be pressure on the nerve root.

A laminectomy procedure usually lasts about an hour and a half. The time spent in the operating room will be somewhat longer, of course, because of the time taken for induction of anesthesia. Afterward, the patient spends some time in a recovery room and it may be at least four hours, sometimes much longer, before the family can visit him.

Generally, the hospital stay is about ten days, allowing time for the wound to heal and stitches to be removed, although some neurosurgeons now send patients home with stitches still in place and remove them later during an office visit.

After surgery activity must be restricted long enough to allow complete healing of tissues. Usually, after a laminectomy, a patient is able to undertake light activities within three weeks. The time for return to full-time work depends upon the type of work. The patient who works at a desk and has occasion to lift only very light objects will be able to go back to work without discomfort much earlier than, for example, a longshoreman who must lift objects weighing as much as 100 pounds. Even if deconditioned, a man who does light work will usually be able to go back to it without need for pain-relievers. The heavy worker, even after a short period in bed, will need time to reverse the adverse deconditioning effects of bed rest in addition to needing time for healing of the surgical wound.

Sometimes, surgical fusion is required. In fusion, two separate bones are united to eliminate motion at the joint between them. Surgical fusion may be needed when abnormal motion causes pain at a joint. Such motion may stem from arthritis affecting vertebral joint surfaces. Sometimes, degeneration of a disk, with or without compression of a nerve root, may be responsible. Degeneration narrows the space between vertebral bodies. If they come very close together, the small joints between the vertebrae can rub against each other and may cause pain. If there is no evidence of nerve root pressure, then fusion of the two vertebral bodies relieves the pain by eliminating the motion between them.

Occasionally, extrusion of intervertebral disk material causes nerve compression and, in addition, leaves so little of the disk intact that the cushioning effect is lost and pain arises from motion as well as pressure on a nerve root. In such a case, both laminectomy and fusion may be required.

At most large medical centers, laminectomy is usually done by a neurosurgeon and fusion by an orthopedic surgeon. Elsewhere, however, laminectomies as well are performed by orthopedic surgeons, many of whom have had considerable experience and have developed great skill at such work. At New York

University, where it is a rule that laminectomy be done by a neurosurgeon and fusion by an orthopedic surgeon, both surgeons are in the operating room at the same time when both procedures are required.

In a fusion operation, bone surfaces are first denuded and bone chips are then taken either from part of the vertebra itself or from the hip bone. The chips are placed on the denuded surfaces of the two adjacent vertebrae. The bone chips will die; their purpose is to act as a lattice or framework over and through which bone cells in the remaining portions of the two vertebrae can grow. When such bone growth is completed, the two bones have become one.

The bone growth process is much like that in the healing of a fracture; and as with fracture healing, the growth may be slow, and three to six months may be required for solid fusion to be achieved. Also, as with some fractures, bones sometimes do not fuse. Yet, strangely, in some cases of nonunion—and the nonunion can be seen on x-ray—the patient still is relieved of pain. A possible reason for this is that the operation may have led to the laying down of scar tissue which later contracts and may act like a guy wire to prevent motion almost as effectively as fusion. In many cases, however, if there is nonunion, the pain recurs and a new fusion operation must be tried.

As with pain from pressure on a nerve root, sometimes pain from abnormal joint movement disappears spontaneously. When it does not, it sometimes can be reduced or eliminated by preventing joint motion through use of an orthopedic corset.

During the healing period of three to six months after a fusion operation, not only heavy lifting but any excessive motion of the back must be avoided. In some cases, this may require use of a cast.

Generally, a patient's own bone is used for fusion. There is no possibility, then, that the patient will reject the bone, and the results are usually more successful for that reason. On occasion, however, it is necessary to use other bone—from a hospital human bone bank or from specially prepared bone taken from cows or other animals.

Success rates for laminectomy and fusion are difficult to determine. They depend not only upon the quality of the surgery but also upon the accuracy of preoperative diagnosis and the ability of the patient to heal. This may seem like hedging and, to some extent, it is. Yet, factors beyond the control of both surgeon and hospital may play significant roles.

For example, in a totally unrelated procedure, the immediate fitting of artificial limbs after amputation, the same team of New York University surgeons carry out the procedure at University Hospital, which is a private, nonprofit hospital, and at Bellevue Hospital, a public hospital for which New York University provides staff. The technique is most successful at University Hospital but failures have been frequent at Bellevue Hospital. The reasons are fairly clear. First, the nursing care available at Bellevue leaves much to be desired, despite attempts of an overworked staff to do the best they can. Second, the patients at Bellevue usually are indigent, many do not speak English and are poorly educated. Their level of cooperation, therefore, is less than that of the English-speaking, middle-class patients at University Hospital. The nutrition of patients entering Bellevue, and therefore their ability to recuperate, is poor in contrast to those at University.

Similarly, the fusion and laminectomy success rates at one hospital may be distinctly higher than at another, depending upon the quality of surgery and of nursing care, and also depending on the patients themselves. The variables are so great that while overall figures can be given, they provide only a very general idea of what can be expected. Moreover, statistics are of limited use to an individual patient. It is of little importance to a patient if the statistics indicate that 1 out of 10,000 people undergoing anesthesia, for example, will die from the anesthesia. It is most important if he happens to be the fatality. A patient is not so much interested in general statistics as in what will happen to him. Unfortunately, this cannot be predicted with accuracy.

It can be said, however, that given an intelligent, well-nourished, cooperative patient, operated on by an experienced surgeon in a well-staffed and well-equipped hospital where emergencies can be handled (preferably, with interns and residents available around the clock to deal with emergencies), and with a knowledgeable, experienced physical therapy department, the success rate is very high—as high as 90 percent.

In past years, when virtually every pain in the back was considered to be the result of herniated intervertebral disk, the success rate of laminectomies, with or without fusions, ranged down to less than 30 percent. In many cases, there were misdiagnoses; the patients did not, in fact, have herniated disks, surgery could not possibly have a beneficial outcome, and the large volume of such cases confused the statistics.

Today, the whole approach is conservative. Therapeutic measures are tried on all patients prior to laminectomy and fusion. At the very least, a month is devoted to determining whether such measures will eliminate need for surgery. Diagnostic tests, too, are more helpful now. The primary ones are the history, physical examination, and the electromyogram. Myelography is used only to determine precisely where the surgery should be performed and not to determine whether there is a disk herniation or whether surgery is needed. Electromyography and myelography have an accuracy of 85 to 90 percent.

Back pain sometimes may recur after surgery. There may be further extrusion of disk material not removed at surgery. After successful surgery, the other side of the same disk may extrude, or another disk above or below the one on which surgery was performed may degenerate and extrude material, causing nerve root pressure at another level.

Another possibility is that back pain—mimicking the pain of unsuccessful surgery—may develop because of muscle weakness. We are reminded of a patient who had laminectomy and fusion and then, because of continued pain, a repeat operation to make certain that the fusion was successful. The patient could not work for several years, and when we saw him, he had a protuberant abdomen and excessive lumbar lordosis caused by weak abdominal muscles.

He had to be encouraged, almost babied, because he was terrified of any activity, to begin an exercise program. After almost a year of exercises, however, he was free of pain and able to work full-time. It is all too likely that even after successful surgery, back pain—much like what was present before surgery—may appear if weak abdominal muscles lead to excessive strain on back muscles and produce spasm.

It is sometimes possible to avoid surgery and achieve relief of pain associated with a herniated intervertebral disk by injection of cortisone or a related drug into or between the layers of the spinal dural sac. Cortisone and its derivatives are antiinflammatory agents. Compression of a nerve root produces inflammation and consequent swelling. If the inflammation can be reduced—and cortisone provides a means of reducing it—relief, sometimes quite dramatic, may follow. The question is whether this relief is adequate for the long term or whether removal of the cause is preferable. It is a question that must be considered by patient and physican in terms of individual circumstances.

It sometimes happens that a nerve root is compressed as the result of a healing process—one that occurs with advanced osteoarthritis, or wear-and-tear arthritis. The process is called spondylosis, and in it new bone is laid down as a response to wear in a joint. But the new bone mass may develop in such a way that it compresses the nerve root and may then have to be removed by surgery.

Here, as for a herniated intervertebral disk, the indication for surgery may be severe pain that does not respond to an adequate course of conservative treatment or that may respond temporarily and recur repeatedly, leading to incapacitation.

The degree of incapacitation, of course, is something best estimated by the patient. And it is he who, in the final analysis, must weigh such considerations as how much he is willing to pay in pain and suffering from the condition as against the price—in dollars and also in inconvenience and discomfort—of surgery.

There have been preliminary reports recently that in some cases patients wth herniated intervertebral disks may be helped sufficiently by enzyme injection to avoid need for surgery. The enzyme, called chymopapain, is injected into the disk space and apparently can digest extruded disk material. By doing so, it may relieve pressure on a nerve root. Further studies now are in order to determine the effectiveness of the technique when used in a large number of patients and to establish what its value may be over a prolonged period.

As a footnote to this discussion of surgery and the back, we can add a little story, a true one. We often use it at ICD to help illustrate to patients that a herniated or even degenerated intervertebral disk does not inevitably call for surgery, and that without surgery severe limitation of activity is not inevitable.

The medical author's wife has complete degeneration of a disk. She was always an athletic woman in superb condition. Her remarkable muscular fitness suggested that, despite a clear diagnosis of degenerated disk, she might get along well without surgery. She has gotten along well. Only very occasionally is there an episode of pain; it is fleeting and yields quickly to the measures we have discussed previously. Because of the degeneration, she has found it advisable to give up one love, modern dancing. But she continues to ride horseback at least once a week and is an avid skier. Nor has the disk degeneration, which she has now had for more than ten years, interfered with her work, which includes playing with and lifting children.

CHAPTER 11

SEX AND THE BACK

He was a successful 56-year-old businessman who complained of severe back pain which failed to respond to any of the usual measures. For some time, his was a puzzling case. But after getting to know the man well and arriving at the point where we could talk with him in some depth, we determined that his back pain was an excuse to avoid sex with his wife. He had not deliberately settled on it as an excuse; the pain seemed real enough to him. Yet when he came to understand what was going on, he had the courage and strength to face up to the need to resolve rather than avoid his marital and emotional conflicts, and very quickly thereafter his back pain disappeared.

It sounds almost too pat. And yet the fact is that use of some physical problem as a way of escaping an unpleasant situation is not uncommon. It is noted among some sufferers from migraine, heart disease, and many other problems. And back pain, we know from long experience, is commonly used, by both men and women, as a means of escaping having to face up to a disturbing situation, particularly a sexual one.

An awareness of this is important for the solution of many backache problems. Not very often is sexual nor any other emotional difficulty the sole cause, the generator of back pain; but quite often it is a contributing factor or an exacerbating agent. Its resolution by whatever means necessary—by frankly facing up to the situation by the individual or couple, by counseling, or by psychiatric therapy—may contribute significantly to resolution of the backache problem and, of course, to general happiness.

There is another major aspect to sex and back pain. When back pain is severe enough, the usual sexual movements may become virtually impossible. Even when the pain is not very severe, the fear that sexual activity may make it worse can act as a damper or complete inhibitor.

Unfortunately despite all the seeming candor and openness today about sexual matters, sex is still an area full of misconceptions, misinformation, and shyness. It's the rare patient consulting a physician about back pain who brings up the subject of sexual activity, however much he or she may be concerned about it. And many physicians hesitate to bring it up.

This is unfortunate because no matter how serious the back problem, sexual activity is possible—and it is also desirable. It is desirable for many reasons—for the stability of marriage, of course, but also for the release of tensions, both emotional and physical. Such release contributes to general health and makes no small contribution to the health of the back. And the physical activity involved in sex may also help resolve a backache problem.

To set the record straight, there is no cause or factor involved in back pain that is adversely affected by sexual activity. A person with back pain need not fear that sex, somehow, may inflict some permanent damage. The problem, then, lies in finding some way to satisfy, physically and emotionally, both the patient with pain and the partner. And any way may be used if it satisfies both partners and is not offensive to either.

If it is the husband who has the back problem and movement is acutely painful, it may be necessary to abandon the husband-above, wife-below position and allow the wife to be more active. The husband may lie supine with wife above, or the partners may lie side by side and the wife may make the active movements.

If the wife has the back problem, the husband-above position often may be used without discomfort for her if she places a pillow under her buttocks. In many cases, the side-by-side position is most satisfying and least discomforting. Under certain circumstances, the wife may feel more comfortable on her hands and knees with the husband behind her.

If such techniques are not effective, sexual expression of affection is so important and the tension built up in a marriage may be so disturbing if sexual satisfaction is not obtained that it is certainly in order to use mutual masturbatory techniques. They are all the more valuable when preceded and accompanied by warmth and tenderness.

Sexual activity, during an acute back episode and often at other times as well, may be made more pleasurable if the patient's discomfort is reduced prior to going to bed. For this purpose, a hot bath or the application of heat in other forms is valuable. Counterirritants may be used. And if it proves to be helpful, an analgesic may be taken prior to sex—at least 45 minutes before, since that much time may be required for the analgesic to take effect. Gentle massage before sex is comforting for the back and emotionally satisfying as well. It is an excellent prelude to lovemaking.

If, after sexual activity, there should be any muscle spasm, heat, brief massage, and the other techniques described earlier in this book can be used. Much more often, however, the relaxation that follows sexual activity may ease any muscle spasm that may have been bothersome prior to the activity.

Actually, sexual activity at times when acute back pain is not present can be looked upon validly as an aid in overcoming the cause of the back problem and minimizing future attacks of acute pain.

As we have noted repeatedly, the basic need in the over-whelming majority of back-pain patients is to strengthen the abdominal muscles so they can do what they are supposed to do: hold up the pelvis, keep it in line with the spine. When they do this, abnormal strain on ligaments and muscles in the back is reduced or completely eliminated.

Consider the basic movement in sexual intercourse. It is the pelvic thrust. For the thrust, lower abdominal muscles and muscles in the buttocks are used. And it is these muscles that must be strengthened as a prime means of combatting chronic back pain.

For the back-pain sufferer, therefore, the sex act—and its prolongation as much as possible—is, in addition to everything else, an excellent training and backache-preventive aid.

Because satisfying sexual activity is of such great importance to everyone, and certainly to the backache victim and spouse, it is not, we think, out of place to note here the springing up across the country of sexual therapy centers designed to help people with many types of sexual problems—impotence, frigidity, premature ejaculation, vaginismus, and others.

Many are modeled on the famed Reproductive Biology Research Foundation in St. Louis created by Dr. William Masters and Mrs. Virginia Johnson (now Mrs. Masters). These centers offer help that appears to be no less effective than what is found in St. Louis; it is often less expensive and in many cases is available at nominal or no cost to those who need it but have limited or no finances.

By now, the work of Masters and Johnson is well known and needs only brief mention here. In 1966, when the two investigators published their *Human Sexual Response*, it was based on a daring series of laboratory studies of sex. Nearly 700 men and women had been observed during intercourse or masturbation, and the many phenomena occurring in the body before, during, and following orgasm were recorded in detail. New knowledge of sexual physiology, of how the body functions during sexual activity, replaced popular folklore and even much medical mythology.

Not long afterward, Masters and Johnson were able to demonstrate that the knowledge obtained through that study could be applied to helping couples overcome such common problems as impotence and frigidity—and could be applied speedily.

Sexually troubled people, Masters and Johnson found, often shared one thing in common: a tendency to be distracted from natural sexual performance by fears about it. For example, an impotent man, instead of participating unself-consciously in the sexual act, may, in effect, step outside of himself and act much like a spectator, concerned over his ability to have an erection and concerned about what his partner's reaction will be if he fails. His partner does much the same thing. "Neither partner," observed Masters and Johnson, "realizes that the other is mentally standing in an opposite corner, observing the marital bedding scene in a spectator role."

Masters and Johnson based their treatment on two innovations. No matter which partner has the problem, both partners must be involved in treatment; it is the relationship between the two that is the real patient. And the treatment is carried out by two therapists, a man and a woman, each acting, so to speak, as a "friend at court" for the partner of the same sex. A male therapist could best explain a husband's problem to his wife; a woman therapist could clarify a wife's treatment needs for the husband.

In two weeks of intensive therapy in St. Louis, couples who may be referred there from anywhere in the country are educated in how to use the physical senses, especially touch, to give and receive pleasure; they also receive instructions in techniques to be tried in the privacy of their hotel room.

Typically, a couple arriving at the St. Louis clinic is told to refrain from any physical intimacies for the first three days of analyses and interviews. They are then asked to experiment, in the privacy of their hotel room, with touching, stroking and massaging the entire body except for the genitals and the woman's breasts.

It is suggested that the partners take turns lying nude on a bed while the other partner touches, strokes and massages and tries to provide quiet pleasure. For many couples, it turns out, this is really the very first attempt to experience the pleasure of touching and being touched without worry about problems of intercourse.

A few days later, the couple is told to include the genitals in the touching session—and still to avoid intercourse. Very often, by this time, sexual worries have begun to diminish markedly. It is not unusual for an impotent husband, now not having to fret about possible failure, to achieve erections—and for an unresponsive woman, also free of any fear of failure to respond, to actually begin to experience intimations of sexual enjoyment.

Thereafter, the couple is encouraged to go on to intercourse, often using suggestions for positions and manipulations to help overcome a specific problem such as impotence, premature ejaculation, or lack of orgasm in a woman.

Many of the clinics that have been quietly springing up across the country—quite a few in special units in hospitals and medical centers, some in professional office buildings—are modeled on the St. Louis one; some are manned by people trained in St. Louis. Others are being developed by psychiatrists and psychologists not necessarily trained in St. Louis but very familiar with the techniques used there. Many of the clinics have made modifications in the Masters-Johnson technique aimed at making treatment even quicker and more practical for more people.

Treatment is positive, direct, avoids vague generalities—and avoids the depth-sounding, traditional, extended psychoanalytic approach seeking to trace difficulties back to early life experiences.

The aim is to get to the immediate heart of the matter: what is the problem right now? And what can be done, in the simplest way and in the briefest time, to solve or bypass it?

Can such a seemingly serious problem as impotence, long persistent, be overcome after just three brief clinical sessions? This is the record at one of the newer clinics, the Payne-Whitney Psychiatric Clinic of the New York Hospital–Cornell Medical Center in New York City.

How quickly can help be given to a couple with what seems to be a difficult complex of problems: she, a victim of painful intercourse; he, become impotent and full of feelings of guilt and inadequacy after two years of an unconsummated marriage? At a new clinic established at the Long Island Jewish Medical Center in New Hyde Park, there have been many such couples, and almost invariably after nine to twelve sessions they have been able to have intercourse.

All in all, the records of the St. Louis center and the early records of some of the new centers indicate benefits for some 80 percent of patients, a success rate unprecedented in all previous sexual therapy attempts. A partial breakdown shows that treatment has helped 50 percent of men impotent since adolescence; 80 percent of those who became impotent later in life; 80 percent of women who had never previously achieved orgasm; almost 100 percent of men with premature ejaculation problems. While the permanence of these results cannot yet be determined, they seem promising.

It is not our purpose here to go into extensive details about how the clinics help patients solve their problems; much more space would be needed than we have available here.

It is our purpose, however, to point out that it is now increasingly possible for people with any of the common sexual dysfunction problems to obtain help—quick, practical help. And such help is worthwhile for anyone who has a sexual problem, including any backache victims.

CHAPTER 12

HOW TO PROCEED WHEN

ACUTE BACK PAIN STRIKES

You have just come down with an agonizing backache. You may know why; you may not. At the moment, the ultimate cause is not important. In the presence of severe pain, even the most skilled physician would not be able to ferret out the cause and, most likely, would not even try. The immediate, urgent problem is to relieve the pain. How can you best go about doing that?

The important thing to remember is that acute back pain almost invariably is due, entirely or predominantly, to muscle spasm. And so the effort must be directed at relieving the spasm.

The first thing to do is to take two aspirins and get into bed just as quickly as you can. Painful muscle spasm has developed because the body has been called upon—through a sudden motion, accidental injury, excessive bit of lifting or bending, or something else—to take excessive punishment. The muscle spasm provides a painful warning of something wrong; it also is meant to be protective, to splint the affected area and prevent aggravating motion. By getting into bed, you minimize the chance of aggravating motion, reduce demands on the body, and muscles have an opportunity to relax. Even the muscles in spasm relax a bit.

Don't stop at bed rest and aspirins. Remember that spasm in effect feeds upon itself. It causes pain. The pain then can lead to more spasm, and the additional spasm to still more pain, and on and on. The cycle is vicious. The need is to interrupt it. And the earlier the interruption can be achieved, the easier it is to achieve.

Apply heat. Start at once. Use a heating pad wrapped in a Turkish towel. Apply it for half an hour. Then change position so you avoid stiffness.

While most people get most relief from heat, some get quicker relief of spasm and its attendant pain with cold applications. For these people, ethyl chloride or other vapocoolant, if available, should be sprayed on in broad sweeping motions. The stream of ethyl chloride, with the bottle held inverted, should be kept moving. Just beyond the point of burning sensation, there will be a feeling of numbness, and the spraying should continue to this point.

If ethyl chloride is not available, an excellent substitute is gentle rubbing of the painful area with crushed ice or ice cubes in a pillowcase. While the initial shock of cold—a matter of seconds—is disturbing, it is often followed by gratifying relief. It is amazing how many patients, once given an ice massage for an acute attack of back pain, thereafter use it for any subsequent attacks because of the rapidity of action.

As one indication of the value of cold for relieving muscle spasm, a close personal friend of the medical author, Dr. Hans Kraus, who is Associate Professor of Physical Medicine and Rehabilitation at New York University and a world-renowned expert on back ailments who served as one of President John F.

Kennedy's specialists, has remarked that if he were to be marooned on a desert island and could take with him only one physical treatment measure for back pain, he would take a supply of ethyl chloride.

Whether you use heat or cold applications, ask your spouse to give you a rubdown with a counterirritant. Any commercially available counterirritant may do. There appears to be no special advantage to any particular counterirritant. If you should happen to find one unduly irritating for you, switch to another.

Don't hesitate to keep up the aspirin—unless you have some special sensitivity to the drug and have been warned by a physician not to use it; in that case, your physician has probably advised use, when needed for a headache or other pain, of another, nonaspirin type of pain-reliever such as acetaminophen. Use that.

For the vast majority of people, 10 grains (two tablets) of aspirin taken every three to four hours as needed is not dangerous and often is helpful. In addition to its pain-relieving activity, aspirin's antiinflammatory effect is often useful for backache problems.

Repeat the heat or cold applications. If you are using heat and can make it into a bathtub, a hot bath taken for at least half an hour, four or even more times daily, is very much in order. If you can't make it to the tub, keep up the heating pad treatments, alternating with very gentle limbering motions.

Prevail upon your spouse to repeat the massage several times a day. It should be gentle massage, an easy kind of rubbing.

After a day or so, perhaps even overnight, you may notice that the pain is remitting. You may find that you wake from sleep feeling slightly stiff. Motion, very gentle motion—just moving the arms and legs slowly and easily, and stretching and arching and curving the back—will help to reduce the stiffness. Another aid in reducing morning stiffness is to take long-acting, rather than regular, aspirins at bedtime. If you have any muscle-relaxant medication left from a previous episode, you can take that as well.

Next day, continue the aspirins, the heat or cold applications, the massage; and no less often than every half hour, use mobilizing motions.

The mobilizing movements simply involve changing body position—going from a lying-down position to sitting on the edge of the bed with feet hanging down, stretching the arms, gently moving the back, shoulders, arms, and legs. A particularly comfortable sitting position to assume is with hips and knees slightly flexed and the back bent forward.

As pain diminishes a little more, you can proceed to a few other useful exercises. Pull in your stomach muscles, tighten them, hold them that way briefly, then relax. You can do that while lying down. Also while lying down you can reduce the lumbar lordosis, the curve in the small of the back. Simply try to flatten the curve against the bed by leaning slightly forward with your shoulders and pulling in your stomach muscles. Hold this position for just a few seconds. Repeat the two exercises three or four times during each exercise period and go on with them at half-hourly intervals. It is easier with flexed knees.

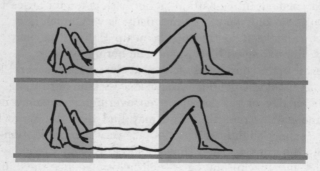

If any movement or exercise should markedly increase pain, discontinue it. A slight increase in discomfort, however, should be tolerated. Only if you "grit your teeth" and continue exercises in spite of severe pain will you increase muscle spasm and pain rather than help reduce them.

It is sometimes helpful in severe cases of back strain to lie either on the bed or on a pad on the floor, with a towel rolled up and placed under the neck, and with buttocks up against the legs of a chair and the feet resting on the seat of the chair. The chair seat should be just high enough to exert a mild upward lift on the hips; if necessary, you can add something atop the seat to increase the height. You can remain in this position for 5 to 30 minutes, until you have maximum relief of pain, and you can repeat the procedure several times a day.

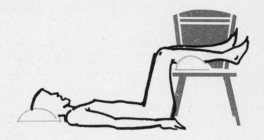

We have been discussing a very severe episode of back pain. Many acute episodes, of course, involve much less severe pain and do not necessarily require bed rest. If a milder episode occurs, you should reduce all physical activities while remaining out of bed, and you can use aspirin, hot or cold applications, counterirritants, and massage. Mobilizing exercises will not be needed since you will not have been at total bed rest.

If you have a severe episode and the pain continues undiminished after a day or so, you should consult your physician. You may need more potent pain-relieving medication or other special measures the physician can provide; there is no need to continue to suffer severe pain.

During an acute episode, pressure on trigger points should be avoided; it may greatly increase the pain and spasm. Only the measures we have mentioned should be used. No diagnostic tests should be tried.

Only when back pain has been reduced to relative mildness is it advisable—or even really possible—to check for cause. At that point, you may wish to explore the possible causes for yourself, using the suggestions in Chapter 3. If you are successful in hitting upon a likely cause, you may then wish to try using some of the measures appropriate for it (described earlier).

If you have any doubts about the cause once a considerable degree of pain relief has been achieved, expert medical diagnosis can be made, and the procedures for that are noted in Chapter 4.

The chances are very great that what will be indicated—by your own or by a physician's diagnosis—is a prime need for a preventive program such as described in the next chapter.

CHAPTER 13

A SIMPLE, EFFECTIVE,

30-MINUTE-A-DAY EXERCISE PROGRAM

FOR TREATING AND PREVENTING BACKACHES

The medical author will never forget the case of a New York City longshoreman, six feet two inches tall, and almost as broad across the shoulders. He weighed 250 pounds and almost all of it was muscle. He came in with severe back pain which had persisted for seven weeks. It was the fourth such episode and every one had been incapacitating.

When, after examining him thoroughly, I told him that his back pain was due to weak stomach muscles, he laughed. "Doc," he announced, "I can lift two of you with each hand." It was only a slight exaggeration. He was accustomed to lifting weights of 100 pounds and often much more many times a day.

Yet, despite his enormously strong back, shoulder, leg, and arm muscles, he had very weak abdominal muscles. Lying supine on the examining table, he could not keep his legs elevated for more than four seconds. He was unable to do a sit-up with knees bent or straight. When I pointed these failures out—as obvious evidence of weak stomach muscles—he remained skeptical.

He was accompanied by his wife, a frail little woman, not much more than five feet tall and weighing less than 100 pounds. I remarked to him: "I haven't examined your wife, since she has no complaints, but I'm willing to bet that her stomach muscles are stronger than yours." The patient laughed and agreed to a small wager.

His wife obligingly got up on the examining table and proceeded, without difficulty, to do repeated sit-ups, with knees bent and knees straight. At that, the longshoreman paled a bit, paid the wager—and, more important, cheerfully undertook an exercise program. He was able to return to work not long afterward. I have not seen him as a patient in the past three years but occasionally get a phone call from him telling me how grateful he is.

Unquestionably, the most important single therapeutic measure for the vast majority of cases of back pain is therapeutic exercise. But there have been many difficulties in getting backache victims to appreciate that fact and to follow through with an exercise program.

For one thing, exercise and activity are not the same, yet they are often confused. Frequently, when exercise is recommended, the patient's response is: "But I am active. Quite active." And there follows a discourse on the activity—sports, housework, gardening, etc.

While it's true enough that many types of activity put various muscles to work, strengthening them (sometimes even to the point of making them bulge), we are concerned here not with muscles in general but with muscles in particular—muscles that must be made stronger to meet specific needs. And backache victims, including many with strong muscles elsewhere, have certain muscles—very often, abdominal muscles—weak enough to lead to their back pain.

There has been another roadblock. While there are some people who enjoy exercising for the sake of exercising—or perhaps more precisely, for the sake of the feeling of being in top physical condition which they get from exercising—they are in a minority. Most people are busy with other matters. Many are lazy. Years ago, at ICD, we found that patients often would be willing enough to do enough exercises to get their pain to go away, but they did not persist with the exercises over the long term. After setting about determinedly to strengthen weak muscles, they were delighted when their work brought them freedom from back pain—but, not very long afterward, their will weakened, they let the strengthened muscles relapse into weakness and suffered back-pain recurrences.

Many exercise programs have been proposed over the years. Most are effective for many people. All stress abdominal strengthening exercises because most people with back problems have weak abdominal muscles. Some of the programs have provided as well for those who have stronger abdominal muscles than back muscles, offering them exercises suited to their particular needs.

But often the exercise programs have been quite involved and ritualistic, requiring at least an hour, and sometimes much more, each day. It is difficult to convince people who must get up at seven in the morning or earlier in order to get to work that it is a joy to get up a whole hour or more earlier and spend the time exercising and, on top of that, to do some more exercising at night before retiring.

In many years of experience at ICD, we have found that most people are willing to persist in exercising provided the exercise program is short as well as effective. And we have arrived at a program that has had gratifying patient acceptance and results.

We recommend that each patient determine his or her major muscle weaknesses and then, using just a few exercises, proceed to overcome the weaknesses. As muscle strength begins to improve, other exercises with greater strengthening effect are substituted, not added. We have found that the substitution rather than addition saves time and leads to improvement at a rate almost as rapid as much more prolonged exercise regimens.

Another means of saving time is to curtail greatly the long warm-up and cool-down periods often called for in exercise programs. It used to be a firm belief that a relatively extended warm-up period—one in which mild exercises are performed slowly—is essential for preventing injury. Warm-up exercises were believed, literally, to warm up the muscles and increase the metabolic rate in muscle tissues. There is, to be sure, some increase in blood flow during warm-up, but this is minor in comparison with the increase associated with more vigorous exercise.

Today, many physiologists believe that a warm-up serves mainly to start the firing of impulses in the nerves controlling the muscles, perhaps reducing somewhat the resistance at the synapses, or junctions, between nerve fibers and between nerve fibers and muscles. This helps in coordinating muscle movements; in effect, it is preparation of the nervous system, and the preparation may be of great value in relatively complex muscular activities calling for a great degree of coordination, as in many sports, for example.

But we have found that it is not essential to spend long periods of time warming up in preparation for exercises to aid back-pain victims. A minute or two is sufficient.

And the warm-up activities need consist only of the gentlest and mildest of movements—turning the head from side to side, wobbling the neck a bit, shrugging the shoulders, raising arms and legs slowly and releasing them, taking a few deep breaths without strain and exhaling slowly, casually tightening arm, leg, and seat muscles.

Cooling off is a process you have undoubtedly witnessed often—as when horses are walked after a race and athletes continue to move about for a time after a race or other event. Cooling off after extremely vigorous activity does help many to avoid muscular cramping. Not all athletes, however, seem to need it.

In any case, the exercises you will be using for your back problem are not so excessively vigorous as to require any extended cool-off period. Just a minute or so of winding down, of repeating the same activities you used for warming up, is usually enough.

After exercising, even if you have not perspired, it is often helpful to take a bath or shower. The warm water helps relax muscles.

You will thus find it possible to encompass warm-up, exercises, and cool-off within a 15-minute time period—with just one or two minutes each for warm-up and cool-off, and the remainder devoted to exercise.

The 15-minute investment in the morning—and ideally the same amount of time invested later in the day, either before retiring or, if preferred, before dinner—is reasonable. We have yet to find a back-pain victim who could not spare that much time.

SOME GENERAL POINTERS ON EXERCISE

Exercises for the back which call for the horizontal position are generally best performed on a relatively hard surface. A firm mattress can be used; even better is a floor with a rug on it.

Strip to underclothes, remove shoes, and, if you like, stockings.

Perform all exercises slowly, rhythmically, in smooth coordinated fashion, with rests between. Avoid jerkiness.

If an exercise produces pain, it may be that you are doing it improperly or that it is too difficult and should be attempted only after less demanding exercises can be performed very easily.

It is a mistake to try to anticipate—to do more vigorous exercises without having made the gradual progression through less demanding exercises. Spasm can develop when muscles are called upon for tasks they are not yet strong enough to undertake. Your purpose is to overcome your tendency to spasm and pain by gradual strengthening of muscles.

It is important to do all exercises with open mouth and regular breathing. *Never* do strenuous exercise while holding the breath. Breath-holding involves closing the glottis of the windpipe, thus making the chest or thoracic cavity a closed cylinder. With contraction of abdominal muscles, the abdominal cavity also becomes a closed cylinder. There is then a rise in pressure in both cavities which can lead to a dangerous increase of pressure within the spinal canal and brain.

Generally, it is advisable to inhale before beginning an exercise and then to exhale while performing the most demanding part of the exercise. Your exhalation should be clearly audible to anyone else in the room. Concentration on exhaling loudly is a good idea.

THE EXERCISES

The exercises from which you will *choose* follow. We emphasize *choose* so you will not be overawed by the sheer number of them. You will hardly be doing all at any one time—and, in fact, may not have to do many at any time.

We will shortly indicate exactly how you can go about choosing those most suitable for you—in short, how you can draw up your own exercise prescription.

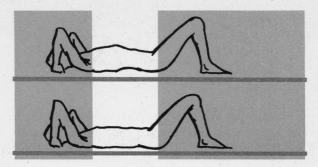

EXERCISE 1. The pelvic tilt. This is a simple yet basic abdominal muscle exercise. Lie on your back on the floor. Squeeze the buttocks together and tighten stomach muscles, sucking abdomen in toward spine and also up toward chest while flattening the back against the floor. Hold the position a few seconds, then relax a few seconds. Flexed knees make it easier.

The exercise also can be done in a standing position, with the back against a wall—and flattened against the wall.

The exercise is actually a step in many of the other abdominal strengthening exercises that follow, and getting the "feel" of it is important. One simple way is to lie on your back on the floor and have a family member slip a hand in the hollow of your back, in the space between your back and the floor. Squeeze buttocks together, tighten stomach muscles, and try to press your low back against the hand. As you tighten your stomach muscles, they may quiver a bit, but this is normal with weak abdominal muscles and should be ignored.

In doing the pelvic tilt, try to equalize the time of muscle contraction and relaxation. Relaxation is important, since during relaxation blood can flow to the muscles, bringing in nourishment and removing wastes.

EXERCISE 2. Tilt and head raise. Lie on back on floor, with knees flexed. While exhaling, squeeze buttocks and tighten

stomach muscles to achieve the pelvic tilt—and, at the same time, slowly raise your head toward your knees. Make the head-raising effort slow and deliberate, and try to raise the head as far as possible with only slight strain.

EXERCISE 3. Single knee kiss. As you achieve proficiency with the preceding exercise—and, in so doing, achieve some strengthening of abdominal muscles—you can move on to this exercise. Again, lie with back on floor and with knees flexed, and do the pelvic tilt, going on then to raise both your head and one knee simultaneously, trying to bring the two together as close as possible. Return to starting position and then repeat with the other knee.

EXERCISE 4. Double knee kiss. As the single knee kiss becomes easy for you to do, substitute this exercise for it. Start as before—on your back on the floor, knees flexed, doing the pelvic tilt—going on to bring both flexed knees toward the chest without raising the head. Briefly hold the knees as close to the chest as you can bring them, then lower them slowly.

EXERCISE 5. Double knee kiss with neck flexed. Repeat the movements of Exercise 4, but now, as you bring both flexed

knees slowly as far as you can in the direction of the chest, also flex your neck and raise your head and shoulders and try to bring head and knees as close together as possible.

EXERCISE 6. Single straight leg raise. This is an important exercise for strengthening the hip-flexing (iliopsoas) muscle.

Begin, as in the preceding exercises, on your back on the floor, achieving the pelvic tilt. Then, with one leg bent at both hip and knee, slowly raise the other leg, with that knee kept straight, to about 30 degrees. The stomach muscles which have been contracted for the pelvic tilt should remain in contraction as the iliopsoas muscle raises the leg.

Do *not* raise the leg beyond 30 degrees. It is at this angle that gravity has the greatest pull on the leg. Raising the leg to vertical position, or 90 degrees, eliminates the gravity effect entirely and makes the exercise much less valuable in strengthening the iliopsoas.

Maintain the leg at the 30-degree angle for 3 to 5 seconds, then very slowly allow it to return to the floor. Repeat with the other leg.

We repeat again the need to do this exercise—and all the exercises—slowly and deliberately. The more slowly an exercise is done, the more difficult it is and the more beneficial. Moreover, there is some improvement in coordination and endurance as well as strength when exercises are performed slowly.

EXERCISE 6a. Single leg raise with weights. Once Exercise 6 becomes easy to do, indicating some strengthening of the hip-flexing muscles, it can be made more difficult—as a means of achieving further strengthening—by adding weights to the feet.

One means of achieving this is with an exercise boot which can be purchased in sporting goods stores and which comes with a range of weights that can be used with it. It is also possible to use your regular shoes and simply tie one or more full food cans (which have clearly marked weights on their labels) or other weights around the shoes.

Start with a 1-pound weight and progress gradually to 5 pounds.

EXERCISE 7. Sit-ups, progressive (A). Sit-ups can be done in various ways so that the exercise can be made easy to begin

with and progressively more difficult and valuable. In all sit-ups, the pelvic tilt is the first step.

In this first and easiest sit-up procedure, lie on your back on the floor, feet straight out so that the knees are straight. You can have someone hold your feet or you can tuck them under some heavy object such as bed, sofa, or bureau. (Commercial exercise boards and tables with straps to hold the feet are available.) Your arms are stretched out, parallel to the floor. Sit up slowly. Avoid a hasty jerking of your weight up, which does not provide the exercise needed. Instead, gradually curl up—raising first head, then shoulders, then chest.

After achieving the sit-up position and holding it briefly, slowly lower yourself down to starting position.

EXERCISE 8. Sit-ups, progressive (B). Repeat all the movements of Exercise 7—but with this single difference. You are lying down in starting position and your arms are crossed in

front of your face with each hand grasping the opposite elbow. This adds just a bit to the work the stomach muscles are called upon to do in achieving the sit-up position and then in slowly returning to starting position.

EXERCISE 9. Sit-ups, progressive (C). Now another bit of progress in terms of increasing the difficulty and value of the sit-ups. You do what you did in Exercise 8—but with one difference. The arms are bent at the elbows, and each elbow is held in the opposite hand, but now your forearms should be touching your waist.

EXERCISE 10. Sit-ups, progressive (D). This is still another step forward, achieved with a change in arm position. Now,

your arms are held so your hands are clasped behind your head,
your forearms are alongside the ears, elbows facing forward.

EXERCISE 11. Sit-ups, progressive (E). As Exercise 10 becomes easy to do, make just another single change in position.
Now, hands are still clasped behind head, but bring the elbows
as far back toward the floor on each side as possible.

EXERCISE 12. Sit-ups, progressive (F). Now, still with feet
supported under a heavy object or by another person as in
preceding sit-ups, but with soles of the feet on the floor so the

knees can be bent to a 45-degree angle (the angle between each thigh and each calf), carry out the sit-ups as in Exercise 11.

EXERCISE 13. Sit-ups, progressive (G). Do the sit-ups as in Exercise 12 but with the knees now bent to 90-degree angle.

EXERCISE 14. Sit-ups, progressive (H). Repeat Exercise 12 with the knees bent enough so that your calves are directly up against your thighs and your heels are against your buttocks.

An Explanatory Note: In doing the sit-ups with your knees straight, you are using your abdominal muscles but also have some aid from the hip-flexing muscles. As you begin to do the sit-ups with knees bent (which automatically bends the hips), you decrease the aid the hip-flexing muscles provide for the abdominal muscles so that the abdominals are called upon for more effort and become increasingly strengthened. The more the hips are bent, the less help from the hip-flexing muscles, until when the hips are bent completely as in Exercise 14, the abdominals are doing all the work.

And when you can do Exercise 14 with ease, you are ready for more advanced exercises for the abdominal muscles.

EXERCISE 15. Sit-ups, progressive (I). Take the same starting position as in Exercise 11. Your hands are clasped behind your head, elbows as far back on each side as possible. Your feet are supported and positioned straight out, with knees straight.

Now twist your upper body so that arms and shoulders are turned to the right. Then sit up, all the time maintaining the twisted position of the upper body. Return to original position. Repeat with upper body turned to the left.

With this exercise, you are strengthening the oblique fibers of abdominal muscles—the fibers running at an angle.

EXERCISE 16. Sit-ups, progressive (J). Return again to the position in Exercise 11—hands clasped behind head, elbows far back on each side, feet supported, knees straight. But now hold a 1-pound weight—a food can or something else—between your clasped hands.

As the sit-ups become easy to do with a 1-pound weight, increase the weight to 2 pounds, and then progressively up to 5 pounds.

EXERCISE 17. Sit-ups, progressive (K). Do Exercise 12 with weights—starting with 1 pound and moving progressively up to 5 pounds.

EXERCISE 18. Sit-ups, progressive (L). Do Exercise 13 with weights—starting with 1 pound and moving progressively up to 5 pounds.

EXERCISE 19. Sit-ups, progressive (M). Do Exercise 14 with weights—starting with 1 pound and moving progressively up to 5 pounds.

EXERCISE 20. Sit-ups, progressive (N). Do Exercise 15 with weights—starting with 1 pound and moving progressively up to 5 pounds.

EXERCISE 21. Sit-ups, progressive (O). Do Exercise 7 except that now there should be no support for the feet. You should be able to do this if all of the preceding sit-up exercises have become easy for you to do. If you are unable to do Exercise 7 without support for the feet at this point, drop back to and continue with Exercise 20 for a time, then try again.

EXERCISE 22. Sit-ups, progressive (P . . .). Once you are able to achieve Exercise 21 without difficulty, you are ready to go on to do the other sit-up exercises—from 8 through 20—all with no support for the feet.

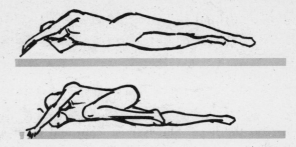

EXERCISE 23. Knee to chest, on side. Lie on your side, with bottom leg bent at the knee, upper leg straight. Bring the upper leg toward the head as you bring the head toward the leg. Try to bring the two as close together as possible. Repeat, lying on the other side, moving the other leg.

EXERCISE 24. Arm raise. Lie prone, with a pillow under the hips. Raise one arm as high as possible, straight above the head, keeping the elbow straight. Relax. Repeat with other arm.

EXERCISE 25. Double arm raise. Assume the same starting position as for Exercise 24, prone, with pillow under hips. Raise both arms together as high as possible, keeping the elbows straight. Lower slowly to starting position.

EXERCISE 26. Chin and chest raise. Lie prone, with both hands behind the head. Slowly raise chin and chest as far as possible. Slowly return to starting position. When this is easy, do the exercise with a 1-pound weight held between the hands and gradually increase the weight up to 5 pounds.

EXERCISE 27. Leg raise, prone. Lying prone, with pillow under hips, raise one leg as far as possible, while keeping the knee straight. Repeat with other leg. If you do this on a bed or on a mattress placed on the floor, you may grip the mattress with both hands while performing Exercise 27.

EXERCISE 28. Double leg raise, prone. Repeat Exercise 27 but now raise both legs, simultaneously, as far as possible.

EXERCISE 29.   Single arm and leg raise, prone. Lying prone, with pillow under hips, raise one arm straight above the head and the opposite leg simultaneously as far as possible. **Repeat with other arm and leg.**

EXERCISE 30.   Double arm and leg raise, prone. Again lying prone, with pillow under hips, raise both arms and both legs simultaneously as far as possible.

EXERCISE 31.   Cat back. Rest on your hands and knees on the floor. Arch your back like a cat while pulling in your stomach so

it quivers and, at the same time, lower your head so you can see your groin. Then bring your head up, looking toward the ceiling, as far as possible; as you do this, you should feel a pull on your back muscles.

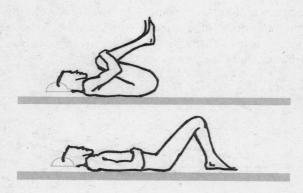

EXERCISE 32. Back stretch. Lying on your back, use both hands to bring your knees close to your chest, and then to squeeze the knees to the chest briefly. With hips and knees still bent, let the soles of the feet down to the floor.

EXERCISE 33. Hamstring stretch. Standing erect, place hands behind buttocks, extend the neck, and look directly forward. Bend at the waist slowly, keeping your eyes directed forward with your head tilted as far up as possible. Bend as much as you can but do not bounce to try to bend farther. As you reach your maximum bending position, you will feel a pulling on the back of the thighs and knees. You are slowly stretching the muscles. If you were to bounce, however, it would cause a protective contraction reaction of the muscles which would eliminate much of the stretching effect of the exercise. This

exercise, which can be repeated a number of times during the day, can be quickly effective in stretching hamstrings.

EXERCISE 34. Heel cord stretch. Tight heel cords, or Achilles tendons, sometimes may be a factor in back pain, especially in

women who have worn high-heeled shoes for prolonged periods. Heel cord stretching is helpful in such cases.

Near a wall, place books on the floor to make a platform 2 to 2½ inches high. Place the balls of the feet on the books. While keeping knees, hips, and back straight, bend the ankles forward so the face touches the wall.

The forward bend of the ankles should be slow and gentle, allowing a steady stretch on the tendons.

EXERCISE 35. Floor touch. Assume the same starting position as for Exercise 33, standing erect, hands behind buttocks, neck extended, looking directly forward. Now, allow the head and neck to droop, and bend toward the floor, feeling a pull on the hamstrings as you do so. Don't bounce; just reach. Some people are able to touch the floor with their palms; everyone should be able to achieve fingertip touching.

EXERCISE 36. Over the table, prone. Bend the upper part of the body over the edge of a sturdy table, so the table edge is at the groin. Grip the table with your hands and, keeping the knees straight, slowly raise the lower part of the body until the

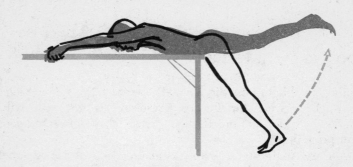

legs point straight out behind you, parallel to the top of the table. Hold this position for 5 seconds, then slowly lower the legs and return to starting position.

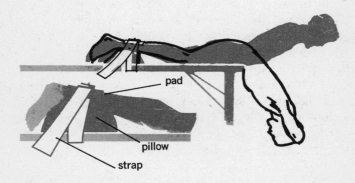

EXERCISE 37. Over the sturdy table, feet held. Start with the lower half of your body prone on a table, the edge of the table at the groin, and with upper body and arms bent toward the floor. While someone holds your feet down, raise back and arms

up until the upper half of your body is parallel to or higher than the table top.

CHOOSING YOUR EXERCISES

If you are unable to pass the Kraus-Weber test No. 1 (see page 74), you have weak hip flexors. Exercises 1 through 6a will strengthen the flexors, and these exercises should be included in your program.

If you are unable to pass the Kraus-Weber test No. 2 (see page 75), you have weak hip flexors and weak abdominal muscles. Your program, then, should include Exercises 1 through 22.

If you are unable to pass the Kraus-Weber test No. 3 (see page 75), you have weak abdominal muscles. Our experience indicates that you will be able to strengthen them most effectively by including in your program Exercises 1 through 22.

If you are unable to pass the Kraus-Weber test No. 4 (see page 76), the muscles of your upper back are weak. Your program should include Exercises 23, 24, 25, 26, 29, 30, 31 and 37.

If you are unable to pass the Kraus-Weber test No. 5 (see page 77), the muscles of your lower back are weak. Your program should include Exercises 23, 27, 28, 29, 30, 31, and 36.

If you are unable to pass the Kraus-Weber test No. 6 (see page 77), you lack sufficient flexibility of hamstring and back muscles. Your program should include exercises 3, 4, 5, 23, 32, 33, 34, and 35.

If you fail more than one Kraus-Weber test, your program should include the appropriate exercises, as indicated above, for the weaknesses you have. If, for example, you fail tests 1, 2, and 3, you should start with the exercises recommended in case of failure of test 1, then move on to those recommended for failure of test 2, and finally to those for test 3. If you fail any of tests 1, 2, or 3, and also fail either test 4 or test 5, complete the exercises for 1, 2, or 3 before proceeding to those for 4 or 5.

In other words, if you fail any combination of the Kraus-Weber tests, do the exercises recommended for failures of the lowest-numbered tests before proceeding to the next higher-numbered ones.

HOW TO PROCEED

Your exercise program should take no more than 15 minutes twice a day—once in the morning, once again later in the day at a time you find most convenient.

In the beginning, for the first day or perhaps for the first few days, you will be experimenting. Begin with the first exercise indicated in your program. If you can do it five times without difficulty, go on to the next. If you can do this one, too, five times without difficulty, you may have time the first day, still keeping within the 15-minute time period, to try more exercises. Repeat exactly the same procedure in the second exercise session later that day. You want to arrive at your proper level, but there is no rush to do so.

Next day, begin with five repetitions of each of the last two exercises you did the previous day, and then go on to the next more difficult.

That day, or the next, or whenever you reach an exercise that is not easy for you to do five times, you will have arrived at your basic starting point.

Once at that point, proceed this way: Begin your exercise period with five repetitions of each of the two exercises immediately preceding the difficult exercise (we can now refer to the latter as the "key" exercise). Do as many repetitions as you can

of the key exercise, then finish your session by doing three repetitions of the two preceding exercises in reverse order. Do exactly the same in the second exercise session later that day.

The following day, again start with five repetitions of each of
the two exercises immediately preceding the key exercise, do as
many as you can of the key exercise, and then do three repetitions of the two preceding ones in reverse order.

Once you can go through five repetitions of the key exercise
without difficulty, you are ready to go on to the next more
difficult one. And you can now begin your session with five
repetitions of the one exercise immediately preceding the former
key exercise, followed by five repetitions of the latter.

Always, no matter how many repetitions of an exercise you do,
carry the exercise out slowly, deliberately. Hold for 5 seconds,
then relax slowly. Take rest time between repetitions, as long a
rest time as the exercise time itself.

You can proceed in this fashion progressively through all the
exercises called for to correct a weakness indicated by failure to
pass one of the Kraus-Weber tests. If you failed more than one
of those tests, you are now ready to begin to correct a second
weakness, and you will proceed in the same way. Now, however,
you will want to maintain the strength of muscles you have built
up. For this, begin each session with five repetitions of each of
the last three—the most demanding—exercises you used to gain
that strength. Then go on to the exercises for correcting the second weakness.

Once you have corrected all weaknesses originally indicated
by the Kraus-Weber tests, you can maintain strength by carrying
out, in each exercise session, five repetitions of the last three,
most demanding exercises in each category. And if you need to
increase strength beyond that because of the demands of your
work and living activities, you can do so by increasing the
repetitions for each exercise—to eight, ten, fifteen, or even
more. If necessary, you can stay within the allotted 15-minute

period by dropping the easiest exercise in each group as you keep increasing the repetitions of the two most demanding.

IF YOU PASS ALL THE TESTS

The Kraus-Weber tests, as we have indicated earlier, are tests of *minimal* muscle fitness. Extensive experience has shown that most people who have at least the level of muscular strength and flexibility required to pass the tests have little or no back pain, while those who fail to pass one or more of the tests tend to have a high incidence of back pain.

But the fact is that some people who may fail to pass one or more, and even all, of the tests do not have back pain, and others who pass them all easily do have back trouble.

As we have pointed out, too, there is no mystery at all about this. If the life a person leads is such that there is very little demand placed upon the muscles, quite weak muscles may suffice. On the other hand, if the life-style is such as to place considerable demand upon the muscles—because of work activities, recreational activities, or any other kind of activities, whether those activities are engaged in frequently or sporadically—more strength and flexibility may be needed than required to pass the tests.

There are also instances in which some structural weakness of the body, even when it is only a minor one, places extra demands on certain muscles and requires that they be stronger than they otherwise would need to be in order to avoid back pain.

If you have back pain and can pass the tests, and if you have not had a thorough medical check before, it is advisable to have such a check. Quite likely, it will point to the need for exercises to increase muscle strength and flexibility well beyond the levels required to pass the tests.

You may well suspect such a need based on the knowledge

you already have about—or a close new look at—your life-style and the demands it places, either day in and day out or only occasionally, on muscle strength and flexibility.

If the need is there, you can make use of the exercises given in this chapter. It is highly likely that you will do well to start with abdominal muscle strengthening exercises, progressing through them all, undoubtedly progressing through the earlier, less difficult ones very quickly. You can increase the number of repetitions of the more advanced exercises for further strength building. And you can go on in the same fashion with the exercises for other muscles.

WAISTBELT EXERCISING (OPTIONAL)

Some back-pain patients like to add to the exercise program the use of weighted waistbelts as a means of achieving day-long "involuntary" exercises.

With a waistbelt, the body's center of gravity is shifted. To maintain balance, the body then must, reflexly, call certain muscles into play. When the weight on the belt is positioned in back, the abdominal muscles must work to maintain balance; if the weight is in front, the back muscles must work.

The belts generally have compartments in which little packets, sometimes containing sand and marked as to weight, can be carried. The belts can be worn under clothing. And many users wear them all day long, at work as well as at home on weekends.

A common mistake is to load the belt with excessive weight. A weight that may seem very light, much too light, early in the morning can come to seem unbearably heavy by midafternoon —for when a belt is worn, muscles are being required to work constantly with little if any relaxation. Sometimes, patients have actually yielded to, rather than keep using their muscles against, the weight, and this may lead to increased pain.

If you want to try a waistbelt, start with minimal weight—no more than half a pound—and work up gradually. It's a good idea to try a waistbelt first over a weekend so you can take it off without delay if necessary.

CHAPTER 14

SPORTS AND OTHER ACTIVITIES

TO IMPROVE BACK AND GENERAL HEALTH

As you gradually strengthen muscles critical in back pain through the exercises you choose for yourself from those listed in Chapter 13, you may want to return to participation in some favorite sport. If you don't already have one, or even several, it would be an excellent idea to look about.

Properly chosen and participated in, sports and other physical activities not only need not bring a return of back pain; they can do much, through further strengthening of critical muscles and through the relaxation and release from emotional and physical tension they provide, to minimize still more the likelihood of back-pain recurrence.

And, at risk of repeating a message most of us have heard often and yet tend to do little about, we urgently need, for general health, to participate more in sports or find other physical activities to use. Ours is an almost incredibly sedentary society. And we pay a high price for sedentary living both in the back pain so commonly caused by inadequate musculature and in overall health.

Lack of physical activity appears to be one major factor in our high heart attack rate and also in the deadliness of those heart attacks that kill. Lack of sufficient activity also contributes to other problems: obesity and the increased risk of high blood pressure, diabetes, and other serious disorders associated often with obesity; strokes that result from the clogging of brain arteries.

Many studies have determined that physically active people are much less prone to heart attacks. In England, bus conductors who move around and up and down double-decker buses to collect fares have fewer heart attacks than the bus drivers, who must sit in one place. Among U.S. railroad employees, the sedentary office workers have twice the heart attack incidence of the men working in the yards. Dozens of other studies comparing active and nonactive people turn up the same consistent finding.

We hear much about cholesterol as a factor in heart attacks, and there is every reason to be moderate in eating cholesterol-rich foods and in avoiding excesses of fatty foods. But it is noteworthy that Harvard investigators studied 700 Bostonians of Irish descent and compared them with their brothers who had remained in Ireland. Coronary heart disease deaths were twice as great in the Bostonians as in their brothers in Ireland—yet the men in Ireland ate more eggs, more butter, more of other fats. Despite their greater consumption of them, however, they had lower blood cholesterol levels. And despite their intake of 400 more calories per day, on the average, than their Boston counterparts, the men in Ireland weighed 10 percent less, on the average. They were getting more exercise and their lower cholesterol levels and lesser weight indicated that physical activity both burns off calories and has a healthy effect on blood cholesterol levels.

It is common to blame obesity on excessive food intake. Yet, very often, the intake is excessive only in terms of the outgo. Take in 3,500 calories more than you expend and you add a pound of body weight. If physical activity is virtually nil, it may take almost a starvation diet to bring down excessive weight and, thereafter, very limited food intake to maintain proper weight. It is much more pleasant to moderate food intake but still enjoy eating while increasing activity—and the increased activity, while helping to bring leanness, can also be counted upon to make you feel more physically fit and healthier.

Recently, in its *Physical Fitness Research Digest*, the President's Council on Physical Fitness and Sports looked hard at the evidence from hundreds of studies on the relationship between exercise and coronary heart disease, and the mechanisms by which physical activity may reduce the occurrence or severity of the disease.

It came to this:

All for the good, on the one hand, physical activity may *increase* the number of extra blood vessels feeding the heart muscle (providing a reserve in case of disease of one of the major blood vessels); it may also *increase* blood vessel size and the nourishment that can be carried to the heart muscle; and it may *increase* heart muscle efficiency and the ability to do more work with less effort. It may also desirably *increase* the efficiency of return to the heart of blood from the extremities, the oxygen content of arterial l lood, the ability of blood elements to minimize or break up clots that might otherwise threaten to block a vessel feeding the heart muscle. And it may also desirably *increase* tolerance to stress, prudent living habits, and joie de vivre.

On the other hand, and also all for the good, physical activity may *decrease* the blood levels of cholesterol and triglycerides, the heart rate, the blood pressure, the stickiness of blood elements, the vulnerability of the heart to abnormal rhythms, obesity, and the strain associated with emotional stress.

THE BACK AND THE MATTER OF ENDURANCE

While one desirable characteristic of muscle is strength, another is endurance—the ability not only to perform but to perform for extended periods. Although endurance often increases to some extent as muscle strength increases, it depends primarily for its buildup on activities that call for continuous effort for a period of time rather than just a few repetitions. Thus, while the exercise program you choose from the series of exercises described in Chapter 13 will build your muscle strength, you can and should increase endurance through sports or other activities, or both.

The activities need not ever involve maximum continuous effort. Certainly at the beginning, the effort should be minimal, though it should be effort for more than a few seconds or even a minute or two. At the beginning, it may be best to limit the time period to 5 or 10 minutes. Later, the time can be extended to 20 minutes or more, and the effort also can become progressively more vigorous.

Actually, when it comes to promoting effective lung function, heart function, and healthy circulation, it is continuous, endurance effort that counts.

Typical of valuable endurance activities are walking briskly, jogging, running, swimming, volleyball, tennis, badminton, table tennis, skiing, horseback riding. While golf is a fun game and unquestionably enjoyable, it usually is of less value because much of the time is spent standing or walking slowly (if one walks at all and does not use a cart).

One activity to be wary of is gardening. Unfortunately, gardening often involves considerable kneeling and squatting, with position unchanged for prolonged periods. As a result, there may be some increase of pain and stiffness.

Among people who love sports, there is some tendency, once an acute attack of back pain is over, to rush right back into a game full blast. Often the result is another attack. Almost invariably, because the pain of an acute attack leads to a reduction in physical activity, general muscle deconditioning occurs, and this must be taken into account.

By all means, go back to your favorite sport as soon as you feel up to doing so—but start in again very slowly and work up to your former level of activity only very gradually. If a prolonged period of bed rest has been needed, it may take weeks, sometimes even months, to get back to your previous physical condition. Athletes are well aware of this and take plenty of time to recoup optimal strength even though they were superbly conditioned prior to enforced bed rest. You should not, soon after a back attack, engage in a team activity that would make it difficult or embarrassing for you to quit whenever you feel strain.

There are advantages to activities such as walking, jogging, running, and swimming for people who have had back pain and, in fact, for many others who must find a way to gradually build strength and endurance. Such activities allow you to start easily, progress at a comfortable pace, and go as far as you like and can benefit from.

Walking is very much undervalued. Any activity that allows you to work up to a point where you begin to feel breathless and may even begin to perspire is an endurance activity. And walking can be very much that. You can start easily—and you can work up to a brisk pace that will make you huff and puff and do a bit of sweating. And, except in the most inclement weather, walking can be done virtually any time, any place, and without need for special equipment.

Much the same is true of jogging and running. You can approach both gradually, starting with walking until you are able to walk quite briskly. You can then begin to intersperse a few brief bursts of jogging, and gradually jog more and more and walk less and less. There is no need, unless you prefer to do so, to go on to running. Jogging in itself is good endurance activity, even jogging in place at home when the weather is bad.

Sports are fine; by all means, find and participate in one you like. But it must be recognized that one difficulty with many sports is that it is possible to get to them only on occasion, perhaps once or twice a week. This is fine as far as it goes—but it is not enough. There should be, if at all possible, endurance activity of some type almost daily. And walking or jogging can be used as a supplement to sports activities.

Actually, almost any opportunity to exercise is worth seizing. Some people, if they choose, have the opportunity to walk up and down steps rather than take an elevator. Most people do not realize that walking down steps has value; they consider walking up strenuous since they get short of breath. And walking up steps is, of course, positive work, since work is defined as moving an object a distance against gravity. Walking down steps is negative work. Yet it is even more difficult for the nerves and muscles, since body weight must be controlled as it is lowered from one step to the next. The leg on the upper step must slowly lower the weight until the lower leg touches the step below.

If you use stair-climbing and stair-descending as exercise, start slowly. Maintain a reasonably erect posture, with no bending at the waist. By all means, run your fingers along the banister so you can catch yourself if necessary—but don't use the banister for support.

Those who excel in sports realize the value of regular activity. The chief of physical therapy at ICD, Theodore Corbitt, is a very young man in his fifties who has run more marathon races than any man in American history. He continues to run marathons at least once a week and recently participated in an invitational 100-mile run in the United Kingdom.

Mr. Corbitt lives near Van Cortlandt Park and runs to work

at 24th Street and First Avenue almost daily, a distance of about ten miles. He works hard physically all day, runs at lunchtime for a while, and generally runs home as well. In addition, each weekend he runs at least one marathon distance of slightly more than 26 miles. Often he does this carrying weights. And he also does exercises daily to strengthen his muscles.

People of any age can often develop surprising physical prowess provided they start slowly and progress gradually. Trouble develops only when those who are deconditioned try to do too much too fast.

It sometimes takes a bit of nudging and some overcoming of preconceived notions to find a sport with which you can be happy. The medical author has to confess that he had great difficulty in finding a sport that he could both like and count on to keep in good physical condition. Fortunately, when he and his bride-to-be became engaged, she thought it necessary to warn him, only half-jokingly, that he would have to learn skiing or she would not marry him.

I had tried skiing when I was a student at Syracuse University and had given it up very quickly. But dutifully I accompanied my fiancée to ski areas week after week and found that I just could not learn to ski. I tried repeatedly to master the snowplow, but because of marked external rotation of the feet (which made me walk almost like Charlie Chaplin), it was a distinct effort to get the skis even parallel to each other and an impossibility to get them into snowplow position.

After about seven weekends of frustration despite the efforts of instructors at various ski areas in California to help, I went to the proprietor of the ski shop at Heavenly Valley in California and said to him: "I recently bought a set of skis and bindings. But my feet point out, so I can't get into the snowplow position and haven't been able to learn to ski. Can you please adjust the bindings so that when I get my feet at least parallel, the skis will be in snowplow position?"

The proprietor looked incredulous. "I've been in this business thirty-five years and never heard anything so stupid," he told me. After a moment of thought, he went on: "I have an idea. Let's talk to Stein Erikson, the head of our ski school."

He took me to Erikson, an Olympic champion who has one of the most magnificent skiing forms of any skier alive. When he heard my story, Erikson almost collapsed with laughter. I seethed; not being able to learn to ski was bad enough; feeling ridiculed made the situation worse.

But Erikson finally got himself under control, stopped laughing, and pointed to his feet. "Look at them," he said to me. They were even more externally rotated than mine. "I can't do the snowplow either," Erikson told me. "I had to learn to ski parallel right from the start."

At the time, that was a revolutionary concept, and while I did not know enough about skiing to realize how revolutionary, he evidently did but had not mentioned it to anyone else. Since then, many ski instructors teach the parallel position and have abandoned the snowplow.

It didn't take me long after that to learn to ski. And with skiing, I found myself in good physical condition from November through May, but not the rest of the year. I tried different sports but it was not until I got to horseback riding that I found one I loved. And although there are people who believe, mistakenly, that riding exercises only the horse, equestrians know better.

A special word about swimming because many backache patients ask about whether it is good for them. Swimming can be relaxing—for both muscle and emotional tension. It is helpful in strengthening back muscles but it has little effect in strengthening the stomach muscles, which very often need buildup if backache recurrences are to be avoided. Swimming in a heated pool can help relieve mild muscle spasm. Most pools and, of course, the ocean are never warm enough for this purpose, and cold-water swimming should be avoided if any muscle spasm is present.

Absence of pain after swimming in cold water indicates that such swimming is permissible. If you are free of spasm, you can try swimming in cold water, and if you can do so without spasm recurrence, fine. Unfortunately, there is no way to tell in advance; it has to be a matter of trial.

One problem with some people who engage in sports is that they take into play the same competitive spirit they display in business and other activities. As a result, for them, sports have little if any real recreational value and may even be harmful when the competitiveness is excessive.

One of my patients, a professional man in his early forties, is a leader in his field and, at work, tends to be quietly relaxed, calm and efficient. He loves handball but whenever he gets onto a court, he immediately becomes tense, worked up, and highly competitive. Despite strong muscles and excellent endurance, he has had frequent recurrences of back pain. I have pointed out the relationship between the recurrences and the stress of competition on the handball court. He understands. And I have recommended strongly that he try to tone down his competitiveness on the court, to play with people who feel no great compulsion to be competitive, and to use handball for exercise, relaxation, and enjoyment. He finds this impossible to do—and continues to have back-pain episodes.

I have another patient, a young stockbroker, who is often under great pressure at work. When he appeared the first time, announcing that he was in agony because of his back, I asked him if he could account in any way for the attack. "I don't know," he told me, "but the market is hectic, my customers are driving me crazy, and, besides, I just lost a game of squash."

He is 32 and in superb physical condition. After examining him, I relieved his muscle spasm with ethyl chloride spray, found a number of trigger points, injected several, and a few days later injected the remainder. Each time we talked about his work and recreational activities. I could not help him with his job problems; his undoubtedly was a high-pressure, tension-provoking job. But it became clear that he carried his tensions and great competitiveness with him onto the squash court, and instead of being a sport that relaxed as well as kept him in good physical condition, squash made him more tense. For him, loss of a game was a catastrophe. He was aware of that even though he was not entirely aware of his tension.

I explained to him the possible effect of tension on the back, urged him to become less competitive on the court and to relax and enjoy the game. He listened, mumbled something, and went on his way.

He was back again within a month with another backache. This time I insisted that he give up squash entirely for at least a month. He protested, but gave it up. Later, he went back, with my approval, to playing squash, but he still has occasional backache episodes when he becomes overly competitive.

None of us is ever going to escape all tension and stress. But even severe stress need do no great harm if we find outlets for the energy the body musters to meet the stress. Without such outlets, the energy has nowhere to go but to churn around and build tension and discomfort. If we allow them, sports and other vigorous physical activities can be of value in many ways, not least of which is in providing relaxation and release from tension.

CHAPTER 15

OTHER SUGGESTIONS

Once you are well embarked on a well-chosen exercise program and are able to add sports and other physical activities, you are, in all probability, a giant stride on the road to conquering your backache problem. There are other measures, often quite simple, and a few or many of them, depending upon individual circumstances, may prove of value.

CLOTHING

Especially in women, clothing may contribute to back-pain problems.

Women with heavy breasts sometimes suffer from severe upper back and shoulder pain, which may radiate into the neck as well, because of the use of brassieres with narrow straps. The straps dig into the skin and muscles. A well-designed brassiere with straps at least an inch wide can avoid this. If only narrow straps are available, sewing onto each of them a piece of stiff material can make for comfort.

Women's shoes often cause problems. High-heeled shoes may allow the Achilles tendons in back of the heels to shorten, leading to pain in the calves, the back, and sometimes even the neck. Very narrow heels tend to cause slight wobbling with each step because of the need to balance on a narrow surface—and this may require excessive muscular activity in walking. It may also make for short, prancing steps which, if fashionable, nevertheless put stress on leg and back muscles.

In a well-fitted shoe, the counter or rigid back part should hug the heelbone firmly enough (but not tightly) so there is no riding up and down with each step, leading to irritation of the heel.

Corsets and girdles, as noted earlier, can be useful in relieving acute back pain because they provide support for weak abdominal muscles. Ideally, corsets and girdles should be worn only in the acute stages of back pain and then only in conjunction with a total program of care, including appropriate exercises. But corsets and girdles should not be worn for the sake of vanity because, as long as they are used and support the abdominal muscles, the abdominals are not used and tend to atrophy and weaken, increasing the likelihood of back pain.

SLEEPING HABITS

If you habitually sleep on your stomach, you may be able to ease or avoid pain by placing a pillow under your hips to relieve the lordosis that otherwise occurs in this sleeping position.

Lying on the side with knees bent flattens the back and is a good position if a pillow is used to support the neck. Sleeping on the back can also be restful and good for the back provided the knees are properly supported, and such support can be provided by placing a pillow under the knees.

STANDING

A proper position during standing can avoid strain. One way to get the feel of what a good stance is like is to stand with your back 12 inches away from a wall. Slowly sit against the wall by bending the knees slightly, perhaps to a 45-degree angle. Now tighten abdominal and buttock muscles, thus tilting the pelvis back and flattening the lower spine. Maintaining this tightening, inch upward against the wall until you are in standing position. Walk about briefly, maintaining the same carriage. Then place your back against the wall again, to see if you have actually maintained the carriage.

For chores that must be done in a standing position, ironing, for example, there is a tendency to assume a swayback position. This can be prevented if you place a footrest under the ironing table and rest one foot on it for a time, then the other foot. In any situation that calls for prolonged standing, you can reduce or avoid excessive strain on the back by bending one knee and hip and putting a foot up on a stool or anything else that happens to be handy. Not for nothing were foot rails placed around saloon bars.

BACKACHES AT THE SINK

Frequently, a backache starts in the midst of some simple act such as brushing the teeth, shaving, or washing dishes over a low sink. A useful pain-relieving measure then—most useful in the bathroom but applicable elsewhere as well—is to raise either leg and rest it on toilet bowl, bathtub edge, or low stool. This flexes the pelvis and acts somewhat like a pelvic tilt to alleviate back pain. It can help very much, too, if you fully tilt the pelvis by tightening abdominal muscles.

What happens when you bend over a low sink is that you require the muscles of the back to support virtually the entire weight of your upper body—about half of total body weight—in bent position, at an angle that may approach 90 degrees. It's a severe strain for the muscles. When you tighten abdominal muscles and tilt the pelvis, you relieve the back muscles of approximately 30 percent of their load by increasing intra-abdominal pressure, which acts as a lifting force.

If pain develops, you should be able to maintain the pelvic tilt for the time you are shaving, brushing your teeth, or washing dishes. You should also remember to do the pelvic tilt during the day as often as possible—while sitting at your desk, walking, having lunch, and at other times. Later in the day, you can carry out your regular exercise program. Often, these measures will be enough. But if the pain does not yield to them, the measures described in Chapter 12 should be used.

LITTLE EXERCISES

Inconspicuous exercises that can be done at various times of the day can aid not only in strengthening critical muscles but also in relaxing them when otherwise, because of tension, they may not be in a state of relaxation.

If a muscle is moved, even quite gently, there is a tendency for it to relax more completely afterward.

Among the most useful of the inconspicuous exercises are the following:

Rotate the shoulders gently, forward and back. Raise them gently to touch the ears and then let them drop back gently. Move your head so you touch your left shoulder with your left ear, then your right shoulder with your right ear. Slowly and gently, turn the head from side to side.

Whenever there is opportunity during the day—standing in

line at a ticket counter, waiting for a traffic light to change, waiting for lunch to be served—tighten the abdominal muscles and hold them tight for a count of six or eight without breathing, then relax them slowly. Occasionally, too, make it a point to breathe in normal fashion with the abdominal muscles contracted, then relax the muscles.

Deep breathing done several times a day is also helpful. Take a deep breath, pull in the stomach, hold the breath with shoulders braced backward; then exhale—and exhale as completely as possible, trying to squeeze all the air out of the lungs, bringing the shoulders forward and depressing them to help make the exhalation complete.

It is worth noting that some recent research indicates that one reason for the cigarette smoking habit may be an unconscious need to breathe deeply. In inhaling a cigarette, many people may be taking a deeper breath than when they breathe normally, and some physicians conducting smoking avoidance clinics now prescribe deep breathing as an aid to overcoming the cigarette habit.

Deep breathing, in addition to expanding the lungs and letting the breathing muscles contract and then relax more completely, may also stimulate other trunk muscles which subsequently may relax more completely.

APPLYING YOGA

Yogic practices may have value in helping backache patients who may be interested in them.

Yoga is a means of obtaining peace of mind and health through meditation. In meditation, the effort is to get down to what is really meaningful in one's life, to get rid of the irritations and frustrations occurring in everyday living, so as to be able to function in a more efficient and happy manner. This can be achieved only with complete control of the body and complete attention to one's deepest self.

Yoga uses a series of postures and techniques to help achieve complete physical and mental relaxation. These postures are assumed through the contraction of certain muscles and the relaxation of others. In changing from one yoga posture to another, previously contracted muscles are relaxed and previously relaxed muscles are contracted. In the process muscle strength and endurance are increased and muscle relaxation is improved. All of this contributes to avoiding back pain. In addition, meditation has a healthy tranquilizing action and serves to add to muscle relaxation.

Yoga has become the object of increased scientific research, and some of the investigations suggest that, indeed, meditative techniques may have practical therapeutic value for a wide range of problems, including control of elevated blood pressure, alleviation of drug abuse, and relief of mental and physical tension. There is nothing of the panacea here, but there appears to be much that can be useful.

Yoga has gone public, so to speak. Started in New York in 1966, the Integral Yoga Institute at first had 250 students. Now there are eleven such institutes in the country, and New York's branches alone have some 3,000 students. In addition, there are hundreds of nonaffiliated yoga groups and classes across the country. Among the students are to be found physicians, psychologists, and others with professional interest in health matters—and, of course, many with health problems.

CHAPTER 16

A SPECIAL WORD ABOUT PREGNANCY AND

POSTPREGNANCY BACKACHES

At this moment, there are about three million women in the United States who are pregnant. Some are having a ball, feeling no discomfort of any kind. But at some point during their pregnancies, many women are likely to know the discomfort of backache.

Back pain, in fact, is so common in pregnancy that most women can be expected to suffer from it to some extent. It is so common that some physicians may even be tempted to consider it virtually a normal symptom of childbearing. But as one obstetrician has remarked, "The pregnant woman, trying to attend to light household duties, pressing her hand to her back while she leans to one side or the other in a futile attempt to ease her pain, is very disinclined to agree regarding its normality."

But if pregnancy backache—and back pain after delivery as well—had to be borne in the past, it does not have to be now.

What causes the backache? As the uterus grows during pregnancy, muscles of the abdominal wall are stretched. The added weight and forward expansion increase the lordosis of the spine, and this in turn leads to further stretching of the abdominal muscles. There is then a tendency of the pelvis to tip forward, producing still more abdominal muscle stretching. With the stretching in front, muscles in the low back contract and become abnormally tense.

As pregnancy progresses, there are changes in hormone levels which lead to a relaxation of the ligaments of the pelvis to permit stretching of the pelvis so the child's head, his largest body structure, can pass through the birth canal. As the ligaments relax, the bones of the pelvis can move against each other. Their rough surfaces may produce some irritation, and muscles respond by tightening up to try to prevent motion. This is most common at the sacroiliac joints, which normally are not movable.

During pregnancy, then, there is considerable extra work for muscles, those of the back in particular. And the load or burden on the back muscles and the likelihood of back pain are greatly increased if the abdominal muscles are weak to begin with.

Also, during pregnancy, there is vascular congestion of the pelvic region and especially of the uterus. The congestion may create a fullness in the back which is responsible for some discomfort. Moreover, the weight of the uterus tends to compress veins, producing some interference with return of blood from the legs, and this may cause some leg swelling and a sense of fullness in the legs and sometimes in the lower abdomen.

With the birth of the child, the uterus is empty but still large. As it begins to shrink, the vascular congestion begins to disappear, but the process takes some time, during which discomfort may persist.

Now, too, unless something has been done about it, the abdominal muscles, weak to begin with and further weakened by the prolonged stretching during pregnancy and the further stretching during delivery, leave the back muscles with excessive load. And now the new mother is usually quite active—diapering and bathing the baby, bending over to pick up the baby. And such unaccustomed activities may contribute to backache.

Thus, there may seem to be a whole complex of reasons why backaches occur during and after pregnancy. Yet the basic problem most often is simply underdevelopment of abdominal muscles.

We have seen such underdevelopment repeatedly at ICD. So have many obstetricians and other physicians. Not long ago, Dr. Evalyn S. Gendel, of the Kansas State Department of Health, undertook a special study with 35 mothers, aged 18 to 23, who suffered from persistent backaches. In no case was there an organic reason for the pain.

Most of the women, young though they were, Dr. Gendel found, had protuberant abdominal walls and ungainly posture. None had participated in sports during school years nor had regularly exercised since leaving school. None engaged in a physically active leisure-time program. And although postpregnancy exercises had been prescribed for them, they had quickly given up the exercising as being "too exhausting." Finally, convinced of the need, all the women undertook a program of gradual physical conditioning which relieved their back pain.

Many women could benefit greatly, could minimize the likelihood of back discomfort during and after pregnancy if they undertook, prior to and during pregnancy, to strengthen weak abdominal muscles, using the exercises for that purpose described in Chapter 13.

What can be done to ease backache discomfort when it does occur during pregnancy?

One useful measure is an exercise designed to realign the pelvis, to return it to more nearly level position. If this can be achieved, then the uterine center of gravity will shift backward, the weight of the uterus will be carried more directly on the pelvic bones, there will be less protrusion against the abdominal wall, and flattening of the abnormal incurve, or lordosis, of the spine may follow.

The exercise, which was developed and tested by Dr. Michael Newton, of the Department of Obstetrics and Gynecology of the University of Mississippi School of Medicine, is simple. It calls for standing 18 inches to 2 feet from the kitchen sink. Bending forward at the hip joints, place the hands on the edge of the sink, keeping the arms straight. While inhaling, raise the hips to increase the lordosis, or incurve of the spine. Then, while exhaling and keeping the knees slightly bent, round the back and tuck the buttocks under.

These movements are repeated three times. Then the hands are dropped to the sides, and an erect position is assumed: shoulders relaxed, knees slightly bent, buttocks tucked under, and the weight carried evenly on both feet—a position in which the pelvis is level.

The exercise is done a dozen times a day—or whenever the sink is approached. And there should be an effort to make the new posture a habitual one.

There have been reports of excellent results in women who have made use of the exercise, with relief of back pain and muscular fatigue and, for many women, a psychological lift as their figures have appeared to be less distorted by pregnancy.

One of the cases reported, a particularly dramatic one, was that of a 28-year-old woman who had suffered backaches ever since childhood and had abnormal sideward curvature of the spine, or scoliosis, as well as lordosis. Childbearing had always greatly aggravated her back pain. She was in her fifth pregnancy when she tried the exercise. Within six weeks, her back pain was gone.

Some reports suggest that the exercise also may be of some value for circulatory troubles. One woman, for example, had suffered painful swelling of leg veins during her first two pregnancies. In her third, the leg problem appeared again, this time accompanied by severe low back pain. After a few weeks of exercise, her back pain eased and, at the same time, her leg problem diminished, permitting her to discard elastic leg bandages.

There are other measures that can be helpful in avoiding or overcoming pregnancy backache.

One is avoidance of excessive weight gain, since the greater the weight, the greater the load on the muscles.

If necessary, especially late in pregnancy, an abdominal support corset may be worn.

It is often helpful when sitting to tilt the back backward so that the uterus is supported more by the back than by the front of the pelvis.

Low-heeled shoes are of value. They may take some getting used to, and it is a good idea to start wearing them from the moment you know you are pregnant.

In addition, if you have long worn high heels, you may benefit by correcting a problem which may be present to greater or lesser degree as the result of their use. You will recall from an earlier discussion that with long-continued use of high heels, there may be shortening of the Achilles tendons at the backs of the heels. The shortening can make it difficult to dorsiflex or bring the foot up. This may produce some discomfort at the backs of the knees and thighs. There may then be a tendency to compensate for this by flexing the knees and hips. This modifies posture and may even lead to pain low in the back.

As we have already indicated, exercises may be used to stretch the Achilles tendons and help overcome the problem. One exercise calls for placing books, enough to make a 2"–2½" platform, about 12 inches from the baseboard of a wall. Face the wall. Keeping knees and hips straight, place balls of feet on the books. Lean forward so your face touches the wall. You will feel some pull on the Achilles tendons. Repeat the exercise as often as you can. After a time, when you feel much less pull, or no pull at all, do the exercise with the feet 18 inches from the baseboard.

Another exercise involves standing 18 to 24 inches away from a wall, facing the wall, with your toes on a telephone directory or book, or anything else that can make a level platform about 2 to 2½ inches high. Place your palms on the wall and, bending

your elbows, lean forward and let your face come close to the wall. You should feel some pulling as the tendons are stretched. Maintain the position for a few seconds, then relax. Repeat this as often as you can during the day.

CHAPTER 17

A SPECIAL WORD ABOUT BACKACHES

IN OLDER PEOPLE

Older people are subject to backaches from all the same causes as younger people; and especially as they become more sedentary and lose muscle strength, they may be all the more likely to have back trouble.

In addition, of course, they have lived longer and there has been more time for degeneration of intervertebral disks and for wear-and-tear arthritis (osteoarthritis) to exert long-term effects. As osteoarthritis progresses, the lubricating surfaces of joints may roughen and grate on each other. Sometimes, the grating can be felt and heard. The roughening and grating develop because of cartilage wear-out. To compensate for the loss of cartilage, new bone may be produced; and with bone touching bone, movement may become somewhat painful. Muscles then tighten up to try to prevent the painful movement; but this muscle tightening, persisting as muscle spasm, can become very painful in itself.

While wear-and-tear and reparative processes cannot be changed, often it is possible to compensate for them by exercise, provided the patient does not have any condition that prohibits such exercise. Actually, it is the rare person who does have such a condition; even for patients who have had heart attacks and for many with severe lung disorders, carefully supervised exercise programs have been shown to be beneficial, helping to improve heart and lung function, general health and well-being, and health of the back.

OSTEOPOROSIS

A common cause of back pain in older people, especially in women, is osteoporosis, or thinning of bone structure.

Bone, although it may appear to be, is not a dense, inert substance. Most of us are familiar, of course, with steak bones and chicken bones, which have a lifeless appearance and seem very hard. We hear of orthopedic surgeons sawing bone, pinning broken bones, using screws and plates to attach bones to each other.

But bone is a living substance which changes more rapidly than most people would imagine. Special cells called osteoblasts lay down added bone when it is needed to meet stresses. At the same time, other special cells, osteoclasts, break down unneeded bone, bone that is not being stressed by muscle pull. The building up and breaking down of bone go on throughout life.

As people get older and become less active, muscle stresses on bone structure decrease. For this reason, the osteoclasts are busier breaking down bone than the osteoblasts are building it up. In addition, in women after menopause, with decline in sex hormone activity there is a tendency for calcium salts, which give bone its rigidity, to diminish in quantity. This leads to a thinning of bone called osteoporosis.

The thinning itself is painless. But if bone becomes very thin, it may develop very fine cracks—tiny fractures—as the result of what otherwise might be only trivial injuries. For example, a car ride over a bumpy road may be enough to produce a small hairline crack in a vertebra in the spinal column. If the crack pulls on the bone covering, the periosteum, there may be severe back pain. The crack may be so minute that it cannot be detected on x-ray, although sometimes, after about six or eight weeks, a thickening of bone at the fracture site may be seen on x-ray.

Osteoporosis today is the subject of increasingly intensive research. The effort is to learn more in detail about the nature of the phenomenon with the hope that ways may be found to prevent it. There is also a major effort to find new and more effective treatments for it.

The problem of finding better treatment measures is complicated by the fact that it is difficult to determine when remineralization of bone—the redeposit of minerals—which would be highly desirable, actually occurs. The opposite process—the demineralization—which produces osteoporosis, apparently goes on over a period of many years before the results become apparent on x-ray examination of the spine. Remineralization may take an equally long period before results show up on x-ray. This slows down the testing and evaluation of hopeful new methods of treatment.

One mainstay of current treatment for osteoporosis is diet. Patients are usually asked to drink at least a pint, and as much as a quart, of milk daily, preferably low-fat or nonfat milk. They are also asked to consume adequate amounts of fruits, vegetables, and cereals. Calcium salts may be used for people who do not tolerate milk well.

Vitamin D may be recommended. The vitamin is a factor in

increasing absorption of calcium from the diet. Vitamin D may be needed especially by people in northern areas who have little exposure to the sun. It should be used with the advice of a physician, not indiscriminately, since excessive amounts of vitamin D are not without danger.

Another supplement to the diet that may be used is inorganic phosphate. This is a newer measure and is based on the finding that phosphate may help to decrease the rate at which calcium is lost from bone.

Another new measure is the use of sodium fluoride. This is the same fluoride found naturally in some public water supplies and added to others as a measure for helping to reduce the incidence of tooth decay. Fluoride produces chemical changes in tooth enamel that help to make the enamel more resistant to dissolution by acids in the mouth.

Some years ago, Harvard University investigators discovered, while carrying out surveys in North Dakota, that women living in regions where the drinking water naturally contains levels of fluoride greater than the levels used in water fluoridation programs for tooth decay control had a record of having far fewer fractured vertebrae and, basically, much less osteoporosis than others living in low fluoride areas. It now appears that 10 to 20 milligrams of sodium fluoride a day—an amount higher than used in fluoridated water but still safe—may be useful in reducing loss of calcium from bone.

For women, replacement of the hormone estrogen during and after menopause, now increasingly employed as a means of minimizing or avoiding menopausal and postmenopausal discomforts of many kinds, may have value in preventing osteoporosis. Estrogen has a stimulating effect on bone.

As it stands now, much can be done to help to at least retard the osteoporotic process and to treat the problems that result from it. Before long, preventive and therapeutic measures may be strengthened further.

Investigators currently are working on many new measures, still considered to be in experimental stages and not yet ready for widespread use. One of these, for example, is the use of calcitonin, a recently discovered thyroid hormone, in conjunction with calcium and phosphorus. In a small group of patients, such treatment has decreased bone pain, increased mobility, and produced general feelings of well-being.

DEPRESSION

Another common factor in backache among older people, and sometimes encountered in younger people, is mental depression. The prevalence of depression among the elderly is readily understandable. Our society is one with high regard for youth and little for the elderly. Our standards—of beauty, of intelligence—are those of youth. The aged, with wisdom and experience, are relegated to the dust heap. Ours is a "use and throw away" society. Older people tend to feel discarded and useless. Many have relatively little to do, few distractions, much time to think about aches and pains. They feel depressed.

Depression may not be the reason for back pain, but it may contribute significantly to it. And, in fact, antidepressant medication, by countering depression, often brings marked improvement in back symptoms.

How can mental depression influence pain in the back? It may possibly do so in other ways, but certainly our experience suggests that depression may influence back pain through poor posture and lack of activity.

Consider how a person's bearing so often reflects his or her mental state. Usually, the cheerful person walks and acts cheerfully, vigorously; the depressed person, on the other hand, tends to have a droopy, slumped-over posture and to be much less physically active.

The posture of the depressed can place abnormal stress on back muscles. When the head tends to droop, upper back and neck muscles have added work. When the upper back droops, low back muscles have added work. One area of the back, sometimes even much of the back, may become painful as the result of muscle spasm induced by abnormal stress on the muscles, all instigated by poor posture stemming from depression.

Depression can be difficult to diagnose. For one thing, feelings can change from moment to moment. Moreover, depression not uncommonly produces a considerable variety of body symptoms: change in appetite, change in bowel habits, sleeping difficulty, headaches. The patient, concerned with such symptoms, discusses these when seeking medical advice and sees no connection between them and his or her mental feelings, and the physician may or may not consider the possibility of mental depression.

Today, fortunately, more and more physicians are alerted to the many guises that depression can take. Still, it is a good idea for anyone with backache, or any other physical problem, to be aware of the possibility that feeling low in the mind may have a bearing on the physical complaint—and to confide in the physician, to bring up the fact that he or she does feel depressed.

Sometimes, mental depression can be subtle. It may develop gradually enough so the individual, in effect, becomes habituated to the depressed state of mind. But spouse or friends may notice a change—a loss of sense of humor, for example. The single most common manifestation of depression is sleep disturbance, particularly the inability to stay asleep once asleep. Another common manifestation is tiredness upon awakening in the morning which is succeeded later in the day by increasing alertness.

Antidepressant medication certainly does not constitute a panacea. But it can be helpful. We have had many elderly patients at ICD, and some young ones, whom we have been able to help to some extent with their back pain by other measures and whom we could help much more when anti-depressant medication was added.

CHAPTER 18

A SPECIAL WORD ABOUT

TENSION HEADACHES, NECK PAINS,

AND WHIPLASH

Of all the many varieties of headache, tension headache is by far the most common. It can be extremely painful. It often feels as if there were a squeezing band around the head, a band being pulled ever tighter. There is also pain at the base of the skull in back.

As the name implies, tension headache is related to tension—emotional and muscular. So, very often, is neck pain, with or without headache. The reason lies with the trapezius muscle, which runs from the middle of the back, up the tips of the shoulders and the neck, and attaches to the occipital protuberances, two projections of bone on the lower part of the back of the skull.

If the powerful trapezius muscle should go into spasm, into continuous contraction, it exerts a strong tug on the periosteal covering of the skull, producing an extremely painful constricting sensation. It is also possible for the trapezius muscle, in spasm, to produce neck pain or pain in the upper back.

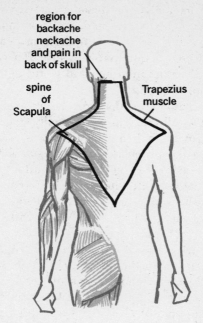

region for
backache
neckache
and pain in
back of skull

spine
of
Scapula

Trapezius
muscle

And the trapezius has plenty of opportunity for going into spasm.

To some extent, humans go through many of the same procedures when under stress as do cats. As a cat, alarmed or disturbed by some situation, gets ready either to pounce or flee, it arches its back and hunches its shoulders. We do much the same, although not so obviously. Commonly, we elevate the shoulders just a bit, enough to contract the trapezius muscle. Any muscle, if contracted long enough, goes into spasm. The trapezius does.

If you tend to suffer from frequent episodes of tension headache or tension neckache, one relatively simple measure can often help reduce the frequency of the episodes. As often as you think of it on any day, and particularly on days full of pressure and stress, take brief time-outs to raise your shoulders close to your ears and then shake them down; wiggle your shoulders and arms up and around, and roll your head around gently in circles. In going through these movements, you are causing muscle contraction but you are also causing muscle relaxation, and the relaxation helps to guard against the development of spasm.

As most people who suffer from tension headaches and neckaches know well enough, they usually get relatively little relief from aspirin alone. If medicine alone is relied upon, what is needed—and what physicians often prescribe for such headaches and neckaches—is an analgesic, aspirin or another, combined with a sedative or tranquilizer, with the analgesic helping to raise the threshold of pain (increasing the amount of painful impulses required before pain is felt), and with the sedative or tranquilizer acting to calm and relax.

Actually, the same physical tools mentioned earlier for relief of muscular spasm affecting the back often can be applied effectively to relieve tension headache and tension neck pain.

Heat or cold may be applied to the trapezius muscle in back of the neck. One or the other may be helpful. If necessary, a counterirritant may be applied, often with more effectiveness after heat application.

Massage is especially useful—and the back of the head and neck is an area you can learn to massage readily yourself. Using the fingertips, rub the area from the back of the skull down the neck and across the top of the shoulders. Repeat a number of times. And, as you feel the area becoming less tender, make large circles with the fingertips around the occipital protuberances, pressing deeply, and then run the fingertips, still pressing deeply, down the neck and across the top of the shoulder on each side. After a few minutes of such massage, spasm should be eased and pain markedly diminished. If necessary, you can take two aspirins. Repeat the massage several times that day; take more aspirin at four-hour intervals if necessary.

And it is helpful, too, to use the relaxation exercises mentioned earlier for helping to prevent spasm—raising shoulders close to ears and shaking them down, wiggling shoulders and arms up and around, rolling head gently around in circles—as an aid in helping to relieve it and prevent its reappearance.

WHIPLASH

One of the most common complaints after a common kind of automobile accident—the rear-end collision—is whiplash injury. While, without doubt, some of the lawsuits over whiplash injury are predominantly financially motivated, the majority have a sound physical basis.

With the sudden jerking or whiplashing of the head in a rear-end collision, there may be stretching and tearing of some of the tissues in the neck—muscle fibers, tendons, ligaments, nerves. Such injuries are often not readily diagnosable by clinical measures short of surgery, which is usually not indicated for them. (If the whiplashing was much more severe than is usually the case, there may be actual fractures and dislocations, with or without paralysis. Such injuries, which can be treated, are outside the scope of this book.)

The difficulty of precise diagnosis in more common whiplash injuries is compounded by the fact that osteoarthritis, the wear-and-tear kind of arthritis, tends to be particularly common in the flexible human neck. Such osteoarthritis can roughen joint surfaces, and the whiplash event may produce a sudden severe scraping of the surfaces which is extremely painful and provocative of muscle spasm.

In addition, there may be small areas of bleeding caused by tearing of muscle fibers. When these areas heal, they heal through the formation of scar tissue which may subsequently tug on surrounding sensitive structures when the neck is turned and bent—and this condition may be permanent.

One of the common measures for treatment of whiplash

injury is use of a cervical collar, which may be made of felt, plastic, or metal. The collar is helpful in relieving pain. It immobilizes the neck and, in so doing, relieves neck muscles of their work. Since they have no work, the muscles tend to atrophy. If the collar is left on for more than a month or so, the muscles may atrophy so much that when the collar is removed, they may find control of head motion too much work for them and they protest in their usual way—by going into spasm.

The natural tendency then is to reapply the collar—which is the wrong thing to do, since it leads to further weakening of the muscles. What should be done is to remove the collar, after about two weeks of use, four times a day and carry out neck muscle exercises. The exercises can be done readily and require no apparatus.

One simple exercise is to place one hand on one side of the face and then use the head to try to move the hand while using the hand to resist the movement. Repeat with the other hand on the other side of the face. You will feel the neck muscles in action.

Go on, then, to place one hand under the chin, with the elbow resting on a chair arm or table. Try to force the chin down against the resistance of the hand.

Place one hand behind the head and use the head to try to move the hand while using the hand to prevent the movement.

Place one hand flat on one side of the head above the ear and try to push the head against the hand as if you wanted to make the ear touch the shoulder, all the time resisting with the hand. Repeat with the other hand on the other side of the head.

A few repetitions of these exercises four times a day after the second week of use of a collar can help to maintain and even increase neck muscle strength. After the fourth week of collar wearing, you may well be able to dispense with the collar except possibly on long trips. You can continue the exercises as long as there is any pain.

Even if you have continuing neck pain resulting from an old whiplash injury, it is worthwhile trying the exercises as a means of strengthening weakened neck muscles and overcoming painful spasm.

Another measure that may sometimes be indicated for relieving continuing neck pain is cervical traction. As we have noted earlier, cervical traction may be carried out at home as well as in a doctor's office. It is often useful for upper back pain and may be equally so for pain entirely localized in the neck (see page 139 for a description of its use).